How to Read a Diary

How to Read a Diary is an expansive and accessible guidebook that introduces readers to the past, present, and future of diary writing. Grounded in examples from around the globe and from across history, this book explores the provocative questions diaries pose to readers: Are they private? Are they truthful? Why do some diarists employ codes? Do more women than men write diaries? How has the format changed in the digital age? In answering questions like these, *How to Read a Diary* offers a new critical vocabulary for interpreting diaries. Readers learn how to analyze diary manuscripts, identify the conventions of diary writing, examine the impact of technology on the genre, and appreciate the myriad personal and political motives that drive diary writing. Henderson also presents the diary's extensive influence upon literary history, ranging from masterpieces of world literature to young adult novels, graphic novels, and comics. *How to Read a Diary* invites readers to discover the rich and compelling stories that individuals tell about themselves within the pages of their diaries.

Desirée Henderson is Associate Professor of English at the University of Texas Arlington, USA.

How to Read a Diary

Critical Contexts and Interpretive Strategies for 21st-Century Readers

Desirée Henderson

LONDON AND NEW YORK

First published 2019
by Routledge
2 Park Square, Milton Park, Abingdon, Oxon OX14 4RN

and by Routledge
52 Vanderbilt Avenue, New York, NY 10017

Routledge is an imprint of the Taylor & Francis Group, an informa business

British Library Cataloguing-in-Publication Data
A catalogue record for this book is available from the British Library

Library of Congress Cataloging-in-Publication Data
Names: Henderson, Desirée, author.
Title: How to read a diary : critical contexts and interpretive strategies for 21st-century readers / Desirée Henderson.
Description: London ; New York, NY : Routledge, 2019. |
Includes bibliographical references and index.
Identifiers: LCCN 2019004674 | ISBN 9780415789189 (hardback : alk. paper) | ISBN 9780415789202 (pbk. : alk. paper) | ISBN 9781315198057 (ebook)
Subjects: LCSH: Diaries–History and criticism.
Classification: LCC PN4390 .H46 2019 | DDC 818/.603–dc23
LC record available at https://lccn.loc.gov/2019004674

ISBN: 978-0-415-78918-9 (hbk)
ISBN: 978-0-415-78920-2 (pbk)
ISBN: 978-1-315-19805-7 (ebk)

Typeset in Bembo
by Newgen Publishing UK

A diary is a dark room that you enter from a brightly lit exterior. It is so dark in there you can't see a thing, but if you stay there for half an hour, you begin to see outlines, silhouettes begin to emerge from the shadows, you begin to make things out. It's like learning a foreign language…

Philippe Lejeune, *On Diary*

Contents

List of Figures ix
Preface xi
Acknowledgments xiii

1 Introducing the Diary 1
Essential Question #1: Is the Diary Private? 19

2 Reading Diary Manuscripts and Editions 23
Essential Question #2: Is the Diary a Feminine Genre? 54

3 Reading the Diary as Literature 59
Essential Question #3: Why Are Some Diaries Written in Code? 91

4 Reading Diary Fiction 95
Essential Question #4: Are Diaries More Truthful than Other Forms of Writing? 125

5 Reading Digital Diaries 128
Essential Question #5: Is the Diary Obsolete, Particularly in the Age of Social Media? 146

6 Why Diarists Write 150

Conclusion: How to Write a Diary 167

Bibliography 170
Index 190

Figures

1.1 *Diary of a Wimpy Kid* by Jeff Kinney. Copyright © 2007 Wimpy Kid, Inc. Used by permission from Amulet Books, an imprint of Harry N. Abrams, Inc. New York. All rights reserved 3
2.1 "Paths to Readers" diagram 25
2.2 Unfolded parcel from Mary Moody Emerson Almanack, 1826. Emerson family papers, 1699–1939. MS Am 1280.235 (385, folders 1–17). Ralph Waldo Emerson Memorial Association deposit, Houghton Library, Harvard University, Cambridge, MA 33
3.1 Molly Lamb Bobak Diary. Molly Lamb enters the Army, November 22, 1942 © Library and Archives Canada. Reproduced with the permission of Library and Archives Canada. Source: Library and Archives Canada. Credit: Molly Lamb Bobak/ Molly Lamb Bobak and Bruno Bobak fonds / e006078933 83
3.2 Takuichi Fujii Diary, 1942–1945. Original caption: "Indeed, this is an odd door. The lock is on the outside. I see that this relocation center is a prison." Courtesy of Sandy and Terry Kita 85
4.1 Page 140 from *Fun Home: A Family Tragicomic* by Alison Bechdel. Copyright © 2006 by Alison Bechdel. Used by permission of Houghton Mifflin Harcourt Publishing Company. All rights reserved 123

5.1 Promotional advertisement for Momento, a diary app launched in 2010. © 2018 d3i Ltd. Used by permission from d3i Ltd 130
6.1 Sample Educational Diary Assignment: "Write Your Life" 163

Preface

My oldest surviving diary is a spiral notebook with a green cover. The metal coil has lost its luster, the paper is yellowed, and the pencil inscriptions are faded. It is not my first diary. At a young age I was given a pink-and-white diary with a tiny gold lock and key – the prototypical feminine diary – but at some point this book was misplaced or thrown away (no great loss, I think). I began writing in the green spiral notebook the summer after I graduated from high school, before I left for college. I was inspired to start keeping a diary because this period in my life felt momentous. I felt like I was at the start of my "real" life – which, at that time, meant an adult life away from the shelter of my family, when I would finally become the person I was meant to be. I did not know when I started writing in the green notebook that I was embarking on a lifelong habit that would eventually become a professional interest as well. Writing a book about diaries was not one of my youthful ambitions but there is no doubt that the many years of diary writing between then and now informs the claims I make within these pages.

This book has two overarching objectives. The first objective is to help readers interpret diaries. This is no small goal because, as anyone who has ever attempted to read a diary knows, diaries are among the more challenging forms of writing. Although diaries have often been dismissed as simplistic or artless forms of self-expression, lacking the complexity of more "highbrow" literary genres, in fact, diaries possess their own complexities.

Following their own internal logic, providing little expository context, employing idiosyncratic writing practices or codes, and often composed over long lifetimes, diaries do not easily admit outsiders. This book seeks to provide the critical contexts and interpretive strategies that will enable readers to not only make sense of a diary's contents but to appreciate its defining conventions, thereby fostering an appreciation of the diary's literary significance.

A secondary goal is to encourage the practice of diary writing or journaling. Many times during the course of writing this book, I mistyped the title as *How to Write a Diary* and I would have to key back and correct myself. But I came to recognize that this typo was an accurate reflection of my hope that readers would be inspired to take up diary writing themselves. Although I encourage a critical approach to the study of diaries, I have an admittedly idealistic attitude toward the practice of diary writing. I sincerely believe it improves individual lives and contributes to solving social ills – which is a great deal to expect from little notebooks filled with personal scribbles. Yet, by exploring diaries written by individuals across cultures, nations, time periods, and identities, I hope to show that this idealism is warranted.

I did not know anything about the literary history of the diary when I started writing in the pages of my spiral notebook. I had never read a diary or a work of diary fiction. The only thing I knew at the time was that my diary was important to me. It gave me a place to think, reflect, dream, and vent that was otherwise missing from my life, a role it continues to play to this day. It was only years later that I came to an understanding of the scholarly debates, key concepts, and analytical approaches that can assist diary readers – and that is what I present to you here.

Acknowledgments

I had the idea for this book while swimming laps at the gym on October 4, 2015, which I know because I recorded it in my diary. The first person I told about my idea was Christopher Conway, whose enthusiasm and encouragement are why the book exists today. Chris has been my sounding board and advocate throughout the entire process, and I cannot fully express my gratitude to him for this – or for all the ways he makes my life worthwhile.

I owe thanks to many people who played a role in the writing of this book: To Faith Barrett, my archival research companion and accountability partner, for her calm, thoughtful guidance. To the other members of my writing group – Theresa Strouth Gaul, Jennifer Putzi, and Alexandra Socarides – for their insightful and rigorous feedback. To Tiffany MacBain and Kathryn Hamilton Warren for generously reading drafts. To my colleagues in the Departments of English and Modern Languages at the University of Texas Arlington for talking to me about diaries, including their own, and patiently answering diary-related questions.

Thank you to Sandy and Terry Kita for permission to reproduce a page from Takuichi Fujii's diary, and to Barbara Johns for her kind assistance.

I am grateful to the editorial team at Routledge including Polly Dodson and Zoe Meyer, and to the anonymous peer reviewers whose feedback assisted this project in numerous ways.

The University of Texas Arlington supported this project with a Research Enhancement Grant and a Faculty Development Leave, and the Department of English provided valuable research funding. In addition, I could not have written this book without the tireless work of the Interlibrary Loan division of the University of Texas Arlington Libraries.

My most significant and heartfelt thanks goes to my students at the University of Texas Arlington, who were the first to read and respond to the material in this book. The students in my 2015 and 2017 courses on life writing were particularly instrumental in helping me shape the book's contents. Their curiosity and excitement about reading diaries convinced me that diaries deserve a more prominent place in twenty-first century classrooms.

1 Introducing the Diary

The most commonly held beliefs about diaries are:

> Diaries are private.
> Diaries are truthful.
> Diaries are feminine.
> Diaries are unliterary.
> Diaries are narcissistic.
> Diaries are obsolete.

Some have described these ideas as myths, and like most myths, they contain enough truth to appear authoritative while greatly understating the complex reality. The pervasiveness of these ideas has led many to dismiss diaries as unworthy of sustained attention or analysis. By contrast, this book prepares readers to critically examine diaries in order to discover how multifaceted they are when not reduced to clichés. In fact, this book argues that what may seem self-evident about diaries turns out to be far more complicated and much more interesting. Reconsidering these characterizations of the diary also necessitates a reconsideration of the genre's prominent descriptors: What is privacy, and why do we expect private writing to be honest and trustworthy? Can autobiographical writing be evaluated for truthfulness when it is filtered through the lens of individual perception or memory? Why are some genres feminized and what are the consequences of this characterization? What kinds of writing get counted as literary, and why? Is self-reflection inherently narcissistic or could it be empowering or healing? Do certain kinds of writing cease to have relevance, particularly when new media become popular? While the primary task of this book is to prepare readers to interpret diaries, answering these questions will allow us to explore many important cultural, historical, and literary issues that have implications far beyond the genre of the diary.

This chapter sets the stage for the project of reading diaries by addressing three foundational topics: the challenge of defining the diary, the origins and history of the genre, and why reading a diary is different from reading other kinds of literature. Although we will move into more complex issues in subsequent chapters, defining key terms and presenting an overview of diary history are important first steps in developing readers' understanding of the genre. I wrap up this chapter by suggesting that, in addition to being intellectually rigorous in our interpretation of diaries, we also benefit from being emotionally engaged and open to the possibility of falling in love with the diary.

Why "Diary"?

In this book, I use the term *diary* instead of the other well-known and related term *journal*. Some people view these terms as interchangeable. Others find it useful to distinguish between them, but there is no consensus among scholars, the general public, or diarists themselves regarding what the two terms mean. For instance, some think of *diary* as referring to more emotionally expressive writing and *journal* as referring to fact-based records of daily life, but others believe the exact reverse is true. Given the instability of these terms, I do not find it useful to differentiate them. Instead, in this book I employ *diary* to refer to the genre as a whole for two reasons. The first is practical: The word *journal* has so many different meanings (referring to periodicals and newspapers, for instance) that it is not particularly useful as a search term. It would benefit readers and the field of diary studies more generally if in the future *diary* were employed as a default label, keyword, and subject heading, making it easier to locate and

Figure 1.1 *Diary of a Wimpy Kid* by Jeff Kinney. Copyright © 2007 Wimpy Kid, Inc. Used by permission from Amulet Books, an imprint of Harry N. Abrams, Inc. New York. All rights reserved

consolidate information and resources. The second reason is conceptual: In using *diary*, I seek to make an intervention, recovering the word and the genre it describes from its status as a feminized, minimized, and even shameful form of writing. The popular children's book *Diary of a Wimpy Kid* opens with the narrator stating, "let me get something straight: This is a JOURNAL, not a diary," and the corresponding illustration imagines him being punched and called a "sissy" for writing a diary (Kinney 1; see Figure 1.1). The text makes clear that the pejorative perception of the word *diary* is linked to misogynist and homophobic attitudes that deserve to be dismantled. I hope to contribute to a reconsideration of these views by exploring how the diary became feminized, why this is considered to be a negative characterization, and how diaries can teach us to rethink entrenched ideas about identity and self-representation. I use *diary* throughout this book in order to destigmatize and normalize the word, affirming its usefulness as a genre designation.

What Is a Diary?

Dictionaries and handbooks of literary terms offer numerous formal definitions of the diary, but let's start with what diarists say within the pages of their diaries.

> A journal is a record of experiences and growth, not a preserve of things well done or said. I am occasionally reminded of a statement which I have made in conversation and immediately forgotten, which would read much better than what I put in my journal. It is a ripe, dry fruit of long-past experience which falls from me easily, without giving pain or pleasure. The charm of the journal must consist in a certain greenness, though fresh, and not in maturity. Here I cannot afford to be remembering what I said or did, my scurf cast off, but what I am and aspire to become. (January 24, 1856)
>
> Henry David Thoreau (American, 1817–1862)

> What sort of diary should I like mine to be? Something loose-knit and yet not slovenly, so elastic that it will embrace anything, solemn, slight or beautiful, that comes into my mind. I should like it to resemble some deep old desk or capacious hold-all, in which one flings a mass of odds and ends without looking them through. I should like to come back, after a year or two, and find that the collection had sorted itself and refined itself and coalesced, as such deposits so mysteriously do, into a mould, transparent enough to reflect the light of our life, and yet steady, tranquil compounds with the aloofness of a work of art. (April 20, 1919)
>
> Virginia Woolf (British, 1882–1941)

> Must I keep filling my small diary with pages of blood? But, Thuy! Let's record, record completely all the blood and bones, sweat and tears that our compatriots have shed for the last twenty years. And in the last days of this fatal

> struggle, each sacrifice is even more worthy of accounting, of remembering. Why? Because we have fought and sacrificed for many years; hope has shone like a bright light burning at the end of the road …. (August 4, 1968)
>
> Dang Thuy Tram (Vietnamese, 1942–1970)

> When the weather was bad, we left the countryside and went in to the nearest bar. There the men started to drink and play cards while waiting for the rain to stop. I would take a napkin and I would write whatever came to mind. The rain stopped and I realized that I was writing a diary. No one can choose what will happen to them in a day, but they can tell it. The diaries of this type are the most diverting way of rewriting that abominable crime that life is. Of recovering it in a selective way. Of turning little things into happenings that are worth thinking about. Before I had not had the opportunity to think about that gray snot that trickles down from my nose when I wash after work. (117)
>
> Rachid Nini (Moroccan, 1970–)*

Is a diary an unripe fruit, a roomy piece of luggage, a blood-stained record, or a soiled napkin? These colorful descriptions convey how diverse diaries are in terms of their form and content, and in terms of the different motivations that drive diarists to write. The idiosyncratic nature of diary writing is one of the things that draws people to the form. The diary accommodates a wide range of writing styles, authorial personas, and individual, social, and political goals. In fact, although some diaries are emblazoned with the word "diary" upon their covers, making identification easy, many are hybrid, multigeneric, multimedia, unstructured, cryptic, and unpredictable texts that may look more like almanacs, account books, commonplace books, photograph albums, sketchbooks, or social media accounts than diaries.

Many scholars have remarked upon the impossibility of articulating a single, reliable definition of the diary genre that

* Translation by Christopher Conway.

can account for such variety. As K. Eckhard Kuhn-Osius states, "It is very difficult to say anything about diaries that is true for all of them" (166). Rather than attempt to create a limiting definition, Robert Fothergill proposes a flexible standard: "let it be agreed that a diary is what a person writes when [they say], 'I am writing my diary'" (3). This approach aligns with two popular theories of genre within literary studies: First, that genres are primarily meant to be functional for human communication or self-expression. Carolyn Miller influentially defines genre as a "social action," writing that "a rhetorically sound definition of genre must be centered not on the substance or the form of discourse but on the action it is used to accomplish" (151). In other words, genres should be defined primarily by the uses to which they are put. Second, that genres are hybrid compositions of other recognizable forms, remixed or repurposed for new goals, and therefore can encompass very diverse texts. Peter Medway coined the term "fuzzy genres" to account for the fact that it is possible for texts that look very different from each other to belong to the same genre (141). The diary is without a doubt both an action meant to accomplish something for diarists and a fuzzy genre that borrows from many different, preexisting forms. Yet the lack of clear parameters when defining the diary also presents some challenges.

On a practical level, the difficulty of defining the diary and therefore identifying texts as diaries presents a research challenge. The ways in which texts are categorized or labeled has consequences for students, researchers, and general readers alike, especially in an era that depends upon keyword searching. If you conduct a search that employs the word "diary," the results will be determined by different interpretations of the search term and by algorithms that use rather than interrogate the myths associated with the genre. At the same time, the difficulty of answering the basic question, "What is this text?," can morph into another, more ideological question: "Is this text important?" The latter is an evaluative question regarding the significance or merit of the text and one that has implications for both archival preservation and the writing of literary history. A text that is not easily classifiable may also be one that is not easily appreciated and it may, as a result, be discarded, destroyed, or ignored, producing gaps in the archive or in the historical record. The question of whether or not a diary is a "good" diary and therefore worthy of preservation within an archive, inclusion in educational curriculum, a place in the canon of literature, or importance in popular discourse cannot be answered without taking into account the influence of entrenched literary hierarchies that often do not make room for hybrid texts that disrupt expectations. I return to these issues in more depth in Chapter 2.

Given these challenges, a caution is called for. Throughout this book I make overarching statements about the diary, seeking to speak comprehensively about the genre as a whole, but it is necessary to remember that every diary emerges out of a specific nexus of individual experience, historical and cultural context, and literary tradition. Diaries are so multifaceted that every broad claim made about the genre within these pages should be understood to be provisional and will not apply to all diaries. This does not, I hope, diminish the value of attempting to make genre-level claims, but it does mean that they must be understood to be open to question and subject to revision.

Diary Categories

Faced with the difficulty of producing a comprehensive definition of the diary, diaries are often subdivided into smaller descriptive categories. These are sometimes determined by the diarist's practices or self-imposed labels, but they may also be shaped by external forces. For example, diary manufacturers have historically marketed specialized diaries for different audiences or functions, thereby influencing who wrote or in what form. Thinking of diaries according to categories helps readers identify authors' motivations, the impact of different diary formats or mediums, the choices diarists make regarding what to include or exclude, and the meaningful patterns that diarists develop and utilize in their writing. Many diaries will fall under more than one category, once again displaying the flexibility of the genre.

Common Diary Categories: blog, bullet journal, confessional diary, courtship diary, devotional diary, diary app, diary of witness, dream diary, gratitude journal, illness diary, letter diary, pocket diary, pregnancy diary, prison diary, multiyear diary, school diary, sex diary, spiritual diary, travel diary, war diary, work diary, vlog.

The following questions are designed to assist readers in developing a critical awareness regarding the defining features of individual diaries.

Diaries characterized by medium or media. What material form does the diary take? What kinds of self-narration does the form encourage? What expectations or restrictions does the material form impose?

Diaries characterized by subject matter. What primary use does the diary serve for its author? How does this intended use influence what the diarist does or does not write about?

Diaries characterized by time, place, or experience. When or where was the diary written? How do external conditions impact the text's subject matter? In what ways do these conditions determine the beginnings, endings, or duration of the diary?

Diaries characterized by interior or exterior focus. Does the diarist focus primarily upon their inner/subjective world or outer/objective world? How does this orientation influence the subject matter or form?

Diaries characterized by narrative style. What is at stake for authors either utilizing or rejecting a "literary" style of writing that employs conventions such as description, characterization, dialog, metaphor, or plot? To what extent does the diarist employ patterns, repetition, fragmentation, gaps, or abbreviation in their writing? What is the relationship between the diarist's stylistic choices and the form or content of the diary? How has the diary's narrative style shaped its reception or status in literary history?

A Very Short History of the Diary

How did diary writing begin? One account of the history of the diary has been generally accepted as the standard and can be found in most books about the genre. However, this version of diary history has also been criticized for its focus on male diarists and its lack of acknowledgment of non-Western diaries. In this section I briefly introduce the standard history as well as the criticism it has received in order to familiarize readers with these issues.

The most prevalent account of the history of the diary is as follows: Beginning in the sixteenth century, a revolutionary cultural shift occurred in the West that placed increasing emphasis upon the individual. While in preceding eras, a person's sense of self and self-worth was determined by external and communal factors such as family relations, class status, property ownership, or religious identity, over the course of three tumultuous centuries (1500s–1700s), it became more common to believe that each individual set their own course regardless of where they came from, who they were related to, or what segment of society they belonged to. The eighteenth-century Enlightenment is the culmination of this major transformation, and it was during this time that the cultural ideal of individualism gained political power through the formation of democratic governments. Among the many consequences of this newfound appreciation of the individual was the emergence of biographical and autobiographical forms of literature, including the diary. The diary is considered to be one of the most significant literary expressions of this new, modern individual; as Roger Smith states, "A sense of self reached its height in the diary" (55). The diary attests to the importance of the individual life, both confirming and reinforcing the widespread belief that each person's story deserves to be told. Yet, while this idealized self was often presented as universal and representative, in truth it was defined by categories of identity (race, gender, class, religion, nationality, etc.) that limited its relevance to wide segments of the population.

Historians of the diary also attribute the genre's emergence to several sociological, technological, and literary changes in the West. Rising literacy rates, the increasing accessibility of writing instruments such as pen, ink, and paper, and more leisure time to devote to reading and writing are identified as prerequisites for the spread of literary practices like diary writing, particularly among the middle and upper classes. Scholars note, as well, the influence of time-keeping technologies and the standardization of time measurements across the Western world. As Stuart Sherman argues, "a new technology for counting time on clocks emerged simultaneously with a new paradigm for recounting it in prose," epitomized in the daily diary (xi). Some of the earliest textual influences on the diary were those that cultivated the belief that a detailed, continuously updated record was key to a productive life, such as calendars, almanacs, account books, and daily planners. These secular forms were complemented by religious literary traditions that encouraged moral self-scrutiny, as can be seen in the confessional diaries written by European and North American Puritans. Tom Webster characterizes "the solitary discipline of reading, self-examination and diary-keeping" as the "bones of Puritan spirituality" (59). Popular media like newspapers and novels also influenced and were influenced by the spread of diary writing. Sherman writes that the earliest British periodicals took the "diurnal, 'secret' time" of the diary into the public, and established it as "a social practice and cultural rhythm" (25). The rise of the novel in the eighteenth century was also instrumental to elevating the stories of ordinary people's lives. As we shall see in Chapter 4, it is no coincidence that many of the earliest novels were written in diary form, as the two genres borrowed from each other in developing a narrative style for representing the dramatic inner world of the individual.

The publication of diaries is also credited with spreading general awareness of the form, as well as creating an added incentive for aspiring writers to keep a diary. Samuel Pepys (British,

1633–1703) is considered to be one of the most influential early diarists because the publication of his diary in 1825 created a popular appreciation for the genre. The publication of Pepys's diary was preceded by John Evelyn's (published in 1818) and quickly followed by those by other British men including John Wesley (pub. 1827) and Lord Byron (pub. 1830). These diaries form the early canon of the genre and establish its defining characteristics: daily dated entries presented in a chronological sequence; an intermixing of public and private aspects of life; a focus on the diarist's state of mind; and a frankness regarding intimate or private matters. The fact that these diaries were published encouraged many diarists to begin to perceive the diary as a literary form and to adopt a style of "deliberate 'literariness'" in their personal writing (Fothergill 32). Over time, more and more diarists would learn about the diary from published diaries, including discovering techniques for self-expression that they could adapt to their own purposes.

By the nineteenth century, diary writing had become so widespread the era has been described as the "golden age" of the diary (Gay 446). By this time, it was possible to purchase inexpensive mass-produced and pre-formatted diaries at local stationer's shops or bookstores, a phenomenon that Molly McCarthy argues produced a "writing revolution" by making it easy for individuals to take up the habit of daily self-narration (108). Several influential cultural critics identify the prevalence of diary writing at this time as playing a defining role in the formation of the modern self: Philippe Ariès names diary writing as one of six cultural practices that give rise to the very notion of private life and individual subjectivity (5); Peter Gay links diary writing with the emergence of Victorian middle-class identity (451); and Michel Foucault recognizes the compulsion to confess sexual secrets as a feature of modern sexuality (*History* 60). In histories of Western individualism and modernity, the diary is acknowledged as a transformative genre that laid the groundwork for twentieth- and twenty-first century perceptions of the self.

This account of how the diary came to be a well-known and popular form of writing by the modern era has received criticism on a number of fronts. First, this narrative privileges male diarists, placing them in a position of prominence within the genre's history. This practice follows a general trend in early works of autobiography studies, which promoted the idea that the autobiographical self is inherently gendered male, a belief that resulted in the marginalization of women's writing. Similar arguments can be found in historical accounts of the diary, particularly stemming from the claim that Pepys either originated or perfected the diary. Feminist critics have pointed out that many women were keeping diaries before Pepys, including such remarkable figures as Lady Margaret Hoby (British, 1571–1633), whose diary predates Pepys's by over fifty years. For this reason, it has been suggested that women should be credited for creating the diary. As Felicity Nussbaum states, "it is possible that women invented such a form, that they began the idea of private, and later, public articulation of quotidian organization of internal experience" (134). Although the status of the diary as private is debated (a point I elaborate in Essential Question #1), many scholars argue that the diary emerged out of the private or domestic sphere, and was designed to record voices that were not granted access to public forms of speech or writing. Scholars note that Pepys's wife also wrote a diary – although Pepys destroyed it during an argument, an event he records within his own diary without apology (Pepys January 9, 1663). The destruction of Elisabeth Pepys's diary exemplifies a central problem in documenting diary history: The absence of women's diaries makes it difficult to accurately account for the role they played in the development the genre. And, it is important to acknowledge that if silences exist around women's diaries, they are particularly acute when it comes to the diaries written by women of color, working class women, lesbian or queer women, and disabled women. Yet it is also clear that women's diaries, particularly when published, exert a significant influence over the perception of the genre. For example, the diary written by Marie Bashkirtseff (Russian, 1858–1884) is referenced by both male and female diarists as an inspiration and role model, and that written by Anne Frank (German, 1929–1945) is today the best-known and most celebrated diary in the world. Given the male-centered record of the diary's origins, it is ironic that over the course of the nineteenth century the genre became increasingly perceived as a feminized genre, so that today it is a form of writing strongly associated with women – and often stigmatized for this very reason. I discuss the diary's *gender paradox* in greater detail in Essential Question #2. Suffice it to say that historical accounts of the diary that place emphasis upon women's writing present a different picture of the genre's origins than has been generally accepted.

The second prominent critique of the standard narrative of diary history is related to its Western-centric bias. The version of diary history that links the genre with the rise of Western individualism runs the risk of making it appear as if diaries are limited to cultures that privilege the individual, as compared to cultures in which selfhood remains tied to community, family, kinship, region, or tribe. This is a common preconception about autobiographical writing in general: That stories of the self can only be written by authors situated in cultures that foster an individualistic sense of self. Georges Gusdorf infamously stated that "autobiography is not possible in a cultural landscape where consciousness of self does not, properly speaking, exist," an absence he correlates with "primitive societies" (30). Dwight Reynolds argues that this perspective remains predominant within autobiography studies, writing,

> The structural and rhetorical characteristics of the western, chronological, narrative-based autobiography have become the gauge by which scholars seek to measure the level of "self-consciousness" and "individual identity" present in other historical periods and other cultures … The almost inevitable result is that other, particularly nonwestern, forms of autobiography are discounted as immature and underdeveloped, as pale shadows of the "real" or "true" autobiography known only in the modern West.
>
> (19)

A similar set of assumptions can be seen in scholarship on the diary, which is considered by some to be a uniquely Western genre with no recognizable corollaries within non-Western literary traditions. Even scholars who analyze diaries within global contexts often start with the presumption that the diary was an alien genre, imported from the West and only taken up by non-Western writers in mimicry of Western diarists. Writing of South African diarists, Liz Gunner poses the question,

> How does one begin to keep a diary when no one has ever suggested the possibility? What cultural models assist the keeping of a "diary" or "journal" especially if these concepts do not, as yet, exist in your mother tongue?
>
> (155)

Other critics have pushed back against this idea by documenting the presence of diary or diary-like forms of self-narration across the globe, many of which pre-date the best-known diaries in Europe. For example, the Japanese tradition of *nikki bungaku* (diary literature) dates to the Heian Period (794–1185) and produced such noteworthy works as *Kagerō Diary* by Michitsuna no Haha (Japanese, 934–995) and *Sarashina Diary* by Sugawara no Takasue no Musume (Japanese, c.1008–?). These texts share the confessional and autobiographical focus of Western diaries but were often written in a combination of poetry and prose. Scholars debate the extent to which these early Japanese texts are comparable to later diaries. Janet Walker cautions against universalizing genres and argues that reading genres through an intercultural lens should ultimately result in a "revision of Western generic classifications and descriptions" (203). Many scholars concur that identifying autobiographical narratives outside of a Western context is an invitation to rethink entrenched genre definitions. In her study of diary writing in Mali, Aïssatou Mbodj-Pouye articulates the challenges and rewards of this work:

> It might sound paradoxical to explore what 'making the self' means through practices so remote from what would qualify immediately as self-writing. But, precisely because

> they emerge without stable models of self-writing, these practices are an interesting starting point for exploring subjectivities when a space for self-fashioning is not given as such.
>
> (206)

Indeed, because they are not limited to the form of the diary that prevails within the West, global diarists have the ability to create new forms of self-expression that expand our perception of what diaries are or can be.

This brief history necessarily simplifies a complex topic that continues to provoke debate among historians and literary critics. It is useful for diary readers to know the standard account of the diary that has been so influential in scholarship on the genre, while also recognizing that this history can be unsettled by a shift in focus that places different voices and texts at the center. The alternative histories introduced here should serve as an invitation for diary readers to explore various explanations of how, why, and when the diary emerged as a recognizable literary form.

Falling in Love with Diaries

Scholars have long recognized that readers relate to autobiographical writing on a more personal level than they do other literary genres. This is abundantly clear in the intense sense of connection that can develop between readers and diaries. Cynthia A. Huff describes diary reading as a "labor of love" (506), while Valerie Raoul writes, "consuming a private diary entails at least a modicum of identification and sympathy for the diarist" (149). David Patterson claims that, in some cases, a personal response to diaries is an ethical responsibility. He argues that readers, and especially Jewish readers, of Holocaust diaries have an obligation to see themselves within the pages of the diary (15). Nor is such a response limited to nonfiction diaries. Sara Day identifies a corollary form of "narrative intimacy" at work in fictional diaries, which she believes fosters "an emotional bond based on trust and disclosure" between the reader and the fictional diarist/narrator (3–4). These characterizations of diary reading emphasize the emotional or affective quality of the reading experience that can arise from the reader's sense of identification or intimacy with the diarist. Reading diaries may provoke a range of emotional reactions including anger, attachment, compassion, judgment, repulsion, voyeurism, and love, and these responses are legitimate and worthwhile elements of the reading experience.

The sense of connection between readers and diaries/diarists helps to explain why so much academic writing about diaries involves a personal component. Scholars frequently write reflectively about their experiences of discovering, reading, or researching diaries, and in many cases the research narrative turns into a discussion of the scholar's own diary. The preface to this book is an example of this merging of the academic and personal. Writing of her work on American women's diaries, Suzanne Bunkers describes how she initially "envisioned approaching these texts as an 'objective observer'" but quickly discovered "that such a stance was neither possible nor desirable for me as a reader and scholar" (18).

> My own experiences, attitudes and beliefs would inevitably shape my reading and interpretation of another woman's diary or journal. How could it be otherwise? I needed to remember that I owed it to myself and the individuals who would eventually read the results of my research, to be as scrupulous as I could in defining the ways in which my own perceptions have influenced my reading of the diaries and journals in my sample. By so doing I work within a self-reflexive paradigm.
>
> (18)

However, not everyone agrees that emotional attachment is a worthwhile component of diary criticism. Fothergill characterizes this kind of scholarship as having "driveled itself away in affectionate sentimentality" (8). The difference between Bunkers's and Fothergill's positions points toward the larger issues that are at stake in the field of literary criticism regarding whether or not it is appropriate to bring personal experience into textual interpretation.

Incorporating self-reflection into academic writing is a scholarly method known as personal criticism. Such self-referential writing runs against the tradition of objectivity in academic research, a stance long associated with rigor and authority. Within the field of literary criticism, the New Critics promoted the idea that literary analysis was a scientific method and rejected the possibility that a reader's individual, emotional, or aesthetic reactions to a literary text could be legitimate components of analytical work. It is an attitude that has become entrenched in what Rita Felski calls "suspicious reading," the pervasive belief that to "do criticism" accurately or well one must embrace "a spirit of skeptical questioning or outright condemnation" regarding objects of study (2). Yet, as Claudia Tate forcefully states, "When we invoke objectivity and universality, we appeal to power and mystify our personal investments so as to speak for everyone. In doing so, we silence those who cannot make similar appeals" (1147). In rejecting the pretense of an objective and dispassionate critical stance, some scholars have instead argued for the necessity of identifying the personal and political stakes of academic research. Feminist literary criticism has been at the forefront of this practice as feminist critics recognize both the implicit gendering of the detached critical stance and the need to represent the particularities of women's experiences. Acknowledging the value of the personal within critical reading practices also has the benefit of opening up the range of affective reactions readers may experience. No longer locked into a posture of suspicion, readers may instead explore the full range of emotional engagement that texts may provoke, including love. This book prepares readers to conduct substantive and informed textual analysis of diaries, but also invites them to recognize the emotional aspects of diary reading as legitimate responses that can teach us a great deal about how the genre works and why it remains so impactful.

Why Read Diaries?

The overwhelming consensus in many spheres of intellectual thought and public discourse is that diaries are silly, girly, insubstantial, and easily dismissible. This book rejects these common preconceptions and proposes instead that diaries are significant and complex works of literature that challenge readers' expectations. In fact, I believe that the devaluation of the diary is tied to the fact that most readers are ill-prepared to understand the characteristics of the genre. Faced with texts that resist standard interpretive practices, it may be tempting to write off the diary as a whole. This book is for readers who instead want to delve deeply into the challenges that diaries present and thereby to recover voices that might otherwise be lost or disregarded within literary history.

Why read diaries?

Because they tell us stories that are not often told in other forms of literature.

Because they tell us stories in ways that defy our expectations and require us to read differently.

Because, in their refusal to conform to literary norms, they remind us of the amazing capacity of language.

Because many people only had the option of writing diaries, when no other form of writing was available to them.

Because, for many people, writing a diary was their last, most heroic act of witness and resistance.

Because many readers are also diarists, and seeing yourself mirrored in literature is a powerful affirmation.

Because they invite us to experience a deep sense of identification and intimacy – even to fall in love.

For these reasons – and for all the reasons you will discover on your own – diaries deserve to be read. This book is designed to assist you.

Essential Question #1: Is the Diary Private?

The most popular descriptor of the diary is that it is a private form of writing. Yet like so much else where diaries are concerned, what initially appears to be a fundamental truth becomes less reliable when you take a closer look. Often "privacy" is correlated with "unpublished" and it is presumed that unpublished diaries were not intended to be read by others. However, in the past, diaries were often coauthored, shared with friends or family members, read aloud at social gatherings, and copied into letters. Today diaries are posted online and read by millions without ever being published in the traditional sense. These composition, circulation, and reading practices challenge the association between unpublished diaries and privacy.

Published diaries can also destabilize the category of privacy. Some will say that a published diary can still be perceived as private if the author did not intend for it to be published or if they write about personal matters in a transparent way. However, it is not always possible to determine a diarist's intentions regarding publication, nor does the diarist always have the ability to control whether their diary is published or read by others. Equally, writing about private topics is a convention of the genre and may not be an indicator of the diarist's attitude about a reading audience. In fact, diarists who seek to be published have an incentive to reveal secrets or recount intimate experiences in order to be successful authors. Already this discussion has moved from a simple public/private binary toward a range of interrelated and overlapping issues including authorial intent, audience, publication status, and reception.

The social and historical context of each diary should also be taken into consideration, as the concept of privacy is both culturally specific and historically fluid. Simply put, privacy is not a simple or a stable category. The distinction between public and private is constantly shifting in response to widespread social phenomena. Nor is privacy a neutral state. Distinguishing between public and private, and determining who has access to these different spheres of experience, are expressions of political power. Patricia Meyer Spacks helpfully outlines the distinction between "privacy to" and "privacy from": privacy as a condition of "personal control" versus privacy as a condition of "limited access" (20). For example, the diarist Zlata Filipović (Bosnian, 1980–) sought to publish her diary in a deliberate effort to raise global awareness about the siege of Sarajevo, which kept her and other Bosnians trapped and isolated in their homes. It was her status as a private citizen – and especially the fact that she was a teenager – that gave her the authority to describe the everyday experience of people in Sarajevo and, to a degree, insulated her from reprisal. She had *privacy to* represent the war, but *privacy from* actual political or military power. She was trapped in the private sphere but employed a supposedly private form of writing to participate in public discourse. These details point toward the complex nature of privacy. On the one hand, privacy can be a privileged status, related to interiority, leisure, and safety. To be alone in a safe and peaceful space is a luxury denied to many people in the world. On the other hand, privacy can be an oppressive structure, restricting access to places of power and to public discourse. To be prevented from full participation in the public sphere can be a way to disempower and disenfranchise. For a diarist, therefore, to seek to keep their diary private – or, alternately, to reject this common classification – may be tied up with questions of identity, social status, politics, and power.

Despite these complicated variables, the association between diaries and privacy remains an influential concept. Lawrence Rosenwald has identified it as one of the defining myths of the diary genre (10). Some scholars describe diaries as "as if" texts: We read diaries "as if" they were private, even when they are not (Paperno 565). In fact, some of the pleasure of reading diaries derives from thinking of them "as if" they were still private, even after they are published (Hassam,

"Reading" 442). Building on these views, privacy might be thought of as one convention out of many that diarists can adopt, adapt, or reject. Diarists know that readers approach their texts with the expectation of privacy and they use this idea to shape their writing choices. In her analysis of diaries that are published as books or as blogs, Kylie Cardell argues that privacy continues to hold sway even in these public formats. She writes, "The diary is a thoroughly public form for speaking intimately of private experience" (*Dear* 142).

It can be challenging to describe the ways in which the diary both references and disrupts privacy using existing terminology. As we will see in Chapter 5, online writing such as digital diaries require scholars to develop convoluted terms like "publically private" (Lange) and "connected privacy" (Kitzmann, *Saved* 91). However, employing more varied terms will enable greater precision regarding the characteristics we seek to describe when we define a diary as private. This wider vocabulary should enable readers to accurately explain each diary's relationship to the concept of the private diary.

The mood, style, or content of a diary	confessional everyday intimate introspective personal reflective secret
The writing techniques and material practices some diarists employ to limit access to their writing	coded concealed encrypted protected
What is done to diaries, sometimes by their authors and sometimes by others (editors, family members, archives, etc.)	abridged censored edited mediated restricted

Are diaries private? It would be more accurate to say that diaries navigate the expectation of privacy. Some diarists make a concerted effort to keep their diaries hidden or to restrict readers' access to all or parts of their writing through the use of codes or other concealment strategies, but many others have a broad understanding of how and why their diaries might be read by others – including the anonymous reading public. Instead of evaluating diaries for their status within the black and white categories of public and private, diaries teach us that there are many different forms of publicity and privacy, and many different ways for literary texts to engage with these concepts.

2 Reading Diary Manuscripts and Editions

Picture a diary in your mind's eye. Almost certainly you are picturing sheets of paper covered in handwriting, perhaps bound like a notebook, perhaps bearing the word "Diary" in looping script across the front cover and locked with a tiny key. The popular idea that diaries are handwritten documents reflects the historical reality that in the past diaries were written with pen and paper, but the visual iconography carries into the present, when people are just as likely to write diaries on computers or digital devices. In other parts of this book I explore the reasons why readers associate diaries with handwritten paper materials, why this perception is particularly common within diary fiction, and why it persists into the digital age. This chapter addresses the practical challenges of reading diary manuscripts as well as diaries that were once manuscripts but which have been transformed into print or digital editions. Diary manuscripts are important objects of analysis because their physical characteristics present a second layer of communication that supplements or enhances the meaning of the words on the page. Readers need to know how to interpret these characteristics, employing manuscript literacy skills to analyze the material features of the text. But the fact is that most readers will not read manuscript diaries in their original form but instead in print or digital editions. The changes that diaries undergo on the path from manuscript to edition introduce new dimensions to the reading experience that were not present in the original. Just as readers can learn a great deal about a diary from exploring how the diarist composed the manuscript, they can also learn about a diary by examining the changes that authors, editors, or publishers made to the text to produce other editions. Making editions involves a process of modification that is often invisible to readers but that deserves to be revealed and explored because it shapes the reading experience in profound ways.

Diary manuscripts take many possible paths to reach readers. As the "Paths to Readers" diagram indicates, diaries pass through many hands and locations, each of which has the potential to change the text (Figure 2.1). In some instances, diarists grant readers direct access to their manuscripts, while in other instances diarists prepare their diaries for publication themselves, in what are known as self-edited editions. These are perhaps the two most direct paths to readers, but even they may involve significant alterations of the original text, either at an early stage of author editing or a later stage of editing for publication. Other paths are also transformative, and may be more so because of the role that editors or publishers play in producing a new edition. These individuals have their own motives and are the products of their own historical moments, which are factors that can influence how they shape a diary for reproduction. The development of digitization technology means that more and more diaries are available in digital formats that reproduce manuscripts as visual facsimiles but, as we will see, even the seemingly straightforward process of scanning a manuscript is transformative. For the most part, the changes that archivists, editors, publishers, and others make to diary manuscripts are meant in good faith to facilitate access and understanding, but they are changes nonetheless and we should examine them with the same attention to detail that we bring to the diary itself.

I begin this chapter by exploring one of the most influential sites on the path to readers: the archive. Although archives may appear to be neutral repositories for manuscripts, they are in fact complex spaces whose history and politics are hotly debated within critical theory. I provide an overview of these debates before offering a framework for readers exploring original diary

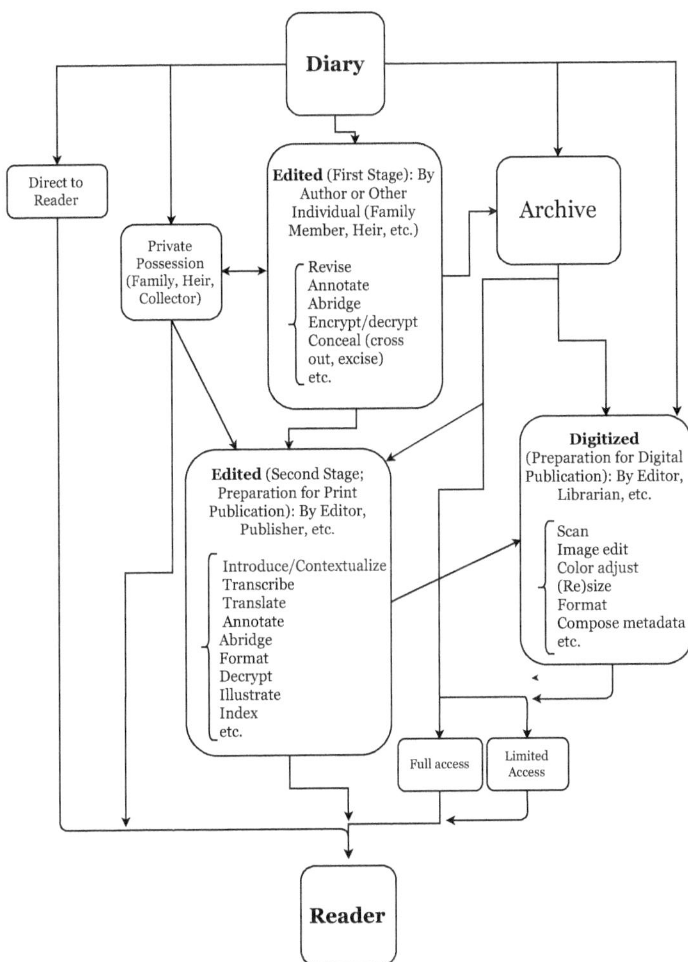

Figure 2.1 "Paths to Readers" diagram

manuscripts and their adaptation into print and digital editions. I identify six of the most common editions in which manuscript diaries are made accessible to readers – facsimile, self-edited, family-edited, mediated, critical, and digitized editions – and assist readers in interrogating how each format shapes the diary's meaning. I close by proposing that students, scholars, and general readers can contribute to the body of knowledge about diaries by producing their own editions of diaries.

The Diary and the Archive

Whether or not a diary was ever held within an archive, the concept of the archive has major implications for the interpretation of diaries. The word *archive* refers to a physical repository for books, documents, and other objects, such as a library, special collections, museum, or historical society. However, as a concept *the archive* refers to a wider set of concerns regarding institutionalized knowledge and the structures of power in society. Although the debates within critical theory around the archive often take on big, abstract questions, they are also linked to the practical act of researching or reading archival documents like diaries. Exploring the archive as a concept prepares us to interrogate the reasons why some diaries are preserved in archives, while others are excluded; how archives participate in upholding or dismantling dominant social norms; and what options are available to readers and scholars who are critical of the archive but still rely on specific archives to conduct research on diaries.

The contemporary critique of the archive originated with the work of two influential French theorists, Michel Foucault and Jacques Derrida. In *The Archeology of Knowledge* (1969), Foucault argued that archives are not reliable collections of documents but rather expressions of prevalent ideologies or systems of belief, concluding that as a result all knowledge derived from archives is contingent. Derrida's *Archive Fever* (1995) applied psychoanalysis to the archive to argue that while preservation is a compelling human instinct, archival preservation is ultimately a tool of social control that determines who can claim and exercise authority.

These two interpretations helped scholars recognize the role that archives have in expressing state power and disenfranchising certain communities. Although archival institutions have historically presented themselves – and are still perceived by some – as neutral repositories that collect and catalogue material, we now understand these archival practices as ways of manufacturing state-sanctioned narratives about truth, value, and meaning. Joan Schwartz and Terry Cook state that archives "actually *create* the histories and social realities they ostensibly only *describe*" (7). Indeed, in failing to preserve or accurately identify documentary records that challenge dominant social norms, archives play a role in silencing certain classes of people and ways of interpreting the world. To exclude something from the archive, as Marlene Manoff writes, is tantamount to excluding it from history (12). Writing specifically of the absence of LGBTQ communities within many archives, Alana Kumbier notes that "when individuals and groups aren't recognized, named, or indexed in library and archival organizing schemes, they are rendered invisible, or are, at least, very hard to find" (114). Such institutionalized practices can result in biased and incomplete historical records, as well as the complete loss of certain voices or stories.

These issues give rise to new approaches to analyzing diaries. For instance, the critique of the archive requires readers to consider whether it is possible to reconstruct a complete and balanced history of a time or place based on the available records. The history of Western colonialism provides a case study of the challenges and rewards of this methodology. There are extensive archival records documenting the spread of colonialism because, as Ann Laura Stoler states, colonial governments are "information-hungry machines" that acquire power through the collection of information ("Colonial" 100). These official record-keeping practices are supplemented in archives by personal and autobiographical documents like diaries and letters written by white Americans and Europeans while they were exploring, traveling through, or living within colonized areas. One of the most infamous examples is the diary of Thomas Thistlewood (British, 1721–1786), a sugar plantation owner in Jamaica whose diary details the violence he perpetuated against enslaved people, including his sexual relations with enslaved women. Many readers have noted the seeming contradiction between Thistlewood's investment in genteel literary practices such as diary writing and his barbaric treatment of enslaved people, but, in fact, his diary demonstrates that the diary could be a tool of colonial rule through which colonizers affirmed the legitimacy of their power and dehumanized colonized and enslaved people.

Thistlewood's diary is an invaluable document for reconstructing the truth of colonialism and slavery but, for readers interested in achieving a full picture of the time, it comes up short because it presents only one side of the story. Archival documents generally present a skewed perspective on colonial history because, while colonized people may be recorded in archival documents, they are rarely given the opportunity to speak for themselves. For readers alert to the politics of the archive, the challenge is to navigate longstanding systems of information in order to uncover those perspectives that are marginalized or obscured. Stoler calls for "reading along the archival grain" or attending to the ideologies that guide archival practices (*Along* 53). In her study of the Caribbean slave archive, Marisa Fuentes reframes this as "reading along the bias grain" or looking for ways of undoing the deliberate erasure of the voices of the colonized within the archive (7). For example, scholars have begun to demonstrate that alongside accounts of horrific violence, Thistlewood's diaries also preserve fragmentary records of the lives of enslaved men and women. Danielle Skeehan has shown that Thistlewood's descriptions of embroidered clothing made by enslaved women provide us with access to "an early example of black Atlantic women's writing" (105).

In addition to developing new ways of reading existing archival materials, scholars also call for finding new materials that record suppressed or forgotten voices. Within the colonial context, this includes recovering first person accounts by colonized or enslaved people. As we saw in Chapter 1, many scholars have assumed that such autobiographical texts simply do not exist, an argument premised upon the belief that autobiography is an essentially Western form of writing. Some early scholars even concluded that the absence of autobiographical writing by colonized individuals was evidence of their lack of civilization or subjectivity. Yet, postcolonial and feminist critics contest this claim by demonstrating that marginalized people have long "manipulated or disrupted the forms that [have] come to be accepted as standard" in order to tell their own stories (Malhotra and Lambert-Hurley 5). Mary Louise Pratt coined the term "transculturation" to describe the process by which the colonized take dominant culture and reinvent it for their own purposes (6). Once again, the diary serves to illustrate how conventional literary forms can function as repositories for alternative stories of the past. The diaries of Amar Singh (Indian, 1878–1942) present a transcultural counter-narrative of British colonial rule of India. As an elite member of the Rajput states of Rajputana, Singh was a "liminal" figure whose ability to navigate between Rajput and British colonial societies enabled him to "reverse the gaze" and resist colonizing narratives (Rudolph 4–5). His cultural liminality is expressed through both the form and content of his diary. For instance, he wrote in English instead of his native tongue, Hindi, but also used his diary to record and celebrate Rajput cultural traditions. Singh's diary stands as a testament to how genres can take on new roles in new contexts. The recovery and preservation of diaries such as Singh's is crucial to ensuring that archives offer a full and complete historical account of the colonial experience, but they may not be easy to find and they may challenge our expectations regarding both genre and identity.

Finally, rethinking the archive calls for the creation of new and more inclusive archives. Activists advocate for members of marginalized communities to develop their own forms of self-representation and preservation, archiving "from the ground up" in order to honor the lives and experiences of community members and to make archiving into a coalition-building activity (Kumbier 117). What new and creative methods could be employed to build more open and egalitarian archives in the future? What would such an archive look like? What kind of diaries might it contain? Although archives are not immune to the politics of different historical moments and can at times become instruments of social control and domination, they continue to play a key role in the production of knowledge because they contain irreplaceable materials, including the traces and fragments that might allow readers to reconstitute a fuller picture of the past.

Reading Diary Manuscripts and Editions

Diaries take many paths to readers and each of those paths creates ancillary information about or around the diary that is worthy of analysis. Reading diaries in manuscript form is only one mode of access but it is a particularly challenging one because it requires readers to have the analytical skills necessary to examine the material characteristics of the manuscript. Reading diaries in print formats may appear easier and more familiar but, in fact, each different edition introduces new layers to the text that deserve to be examined as closely as the diarist's words. Learning how to identify the editorial techniques that were used and the values that determined the editor's decision-making process are techniques that prepare readers to analyze diary editions. Digital editions combine manuscript analysis with editorial analysis, while also introducing a new set of concerns regarding the specific mechanisms and modes of access that digitization employs. This section provides frameworks and reading questions to assist readers in their interpretation of the most common forms of diaries, from manuscripts to print and digital editions.

Diary Manuscripts

Many consider the opportunity to read unpublished, handwritten diary manuscripts to be a privilege. They believe that to hold, touch, and read an original manuscript provides avenues for analysis that are unavailable to readers working with reproductions. Archival documents are often invested with the status of sacred relics that promise unmediated and authentic access to historical truths, with handwritten manuscripts possessing particular power because they impart a sense of intimacy and immediacy by virtue of their closeness to the author's body. As a consequence, reading a handwritten manuscript can be an intensely personal experience and even the challenges of deciphering handwriting can contribute to the feeling that the reader has access to direct and truthful self-representation. The fact that diary manuscripts are material objects – and, for the most part, unique and irreproducible ones – heightens the sense that they communicate as much through their form as through their content.

Readers who have access to diary manuscripts are also perceived as possessing authority as researchers. To conduct archival research is a marker of professional status and accomplishment within many academic disciplines, including literary studies, particularly as most archives are restricted to a privileged few. Even public archives are only accessible to those who can invest the time and money to reach them. The exclusivity of manuscript research is reinforced by the rituals of access enacted in many archives: showing your credentials at the front desk, entering the hushed space, waiting for the text to be brought to you by a librarian, and so forth. The rituals of access enhance the sense that touching and handling a rare material text is a form of embodied knowledge that exceeds what can be known about the text in other formats. Writing of medieval manuscripts, Maura Nolan states that we "cannot learn to read a manuscript in the abstract" (470). The tactile nature of the reading experience relies upon the shape, heft, feel, textures, colors, smells, tastes, and other sensory information conveyed by the text. However, even as we value the experience of reading archival manuscripts, it is important to recognize how this perception reflects the political history of the archive and the ways in which archives contribute to systems of social and class privilege. In other words, just as scholars have challenged the status of "the archive" (discussed in the preceding section), they have also begun the question the academic investment in archival research and to encourage students and scholars to reflect on their preconceptions about manuscripts versus reproductions.

Nevertheless, many scholars contend that studying the original manuscript of handwritten diaries can supplement the linguistic meaning of the written text and, at times, fundamentally alter what is known or believed to be true about a diary. As an example, the diaries written by Hawaii's Queen Lili'uokalani (1838–1917) demonstrate how much the material manuscript contributes to an interpretation of the text. Miriam Fuchs explains that questions have circled around Lili'uokalani's authorship of the book *Hawaii's Story by Hawaii's Queen* (1898) based in part on perceived differences between the writing style she employed in the book versus in the diary she was keeping at the same time, where she wrote in such an abbreviated and fragmented way that some questioned whether she had the ability to write a book. Investigating this question, Fuchs worked first with transcribed and photocopied versions of Lili'uokalani's diaries (the diaries have never been published or digitized). Reading these, Fuchs observed numerous textual characteristics that troubled her and she too began to suspect that Lili'uokalani could not have been the author of *Hawaii's Story*. However, rather than accept this initial conclusion, Fuchs requested access to the original manuscripts, which are kept in restricted archives. She describes seeing the manuscripts for the first time and discovering that Lili'uokalani's chosen medium had profound implications for the diary's contents. What had appeared to be a limitation of authorial voice or style was entirely attributable to the small size and unusual shape of the diaries. Fuchs presents her experiences as a cautionary tale about the dangers of drawing conclusions about diaries without access to the original documents, warning that even seemingly straightforward modes of reproduction such as transcription and photocopying may ultimately "have the effect of distorting the original text."

The personal writing of Mary Moody Emerson (American, 1774–1863) provides another example of how diary manuscripts convey information that might not be possible to perceive without interacting directly with the original text. Emerson practiced a nontraditional form of authorship, writing numerous unpublished volumes she called "almanacks" and which Noelle Baker describes as equal parts almanacs, commonplace books, epistolary essays, and diaries (31). Baker notes that the manuscript form of Emerson's writing gave her the opportunity to communicate through "nonverbal elements" including what are known as "parcels," loose sheets or scraps of paper that Emerson would write on, fold into small packets, and stitch into her almanacks with needle and thread (52; Figure 2.2). Although a digitized edition of Emerson's almanacks is in production, features like the parcels will be challenging to reproduce even in a digital facsimile. It will be particularly difficult to reproduce the tactile experience of unfolding the parcels in order to access their contents, yet surely that experience is crucial to comprehending Emerson's meaning. Folding and stitching may not be typically thought of as forms of authorship, but Emerson's almanacks testify to how material composition practices and the objects they create open

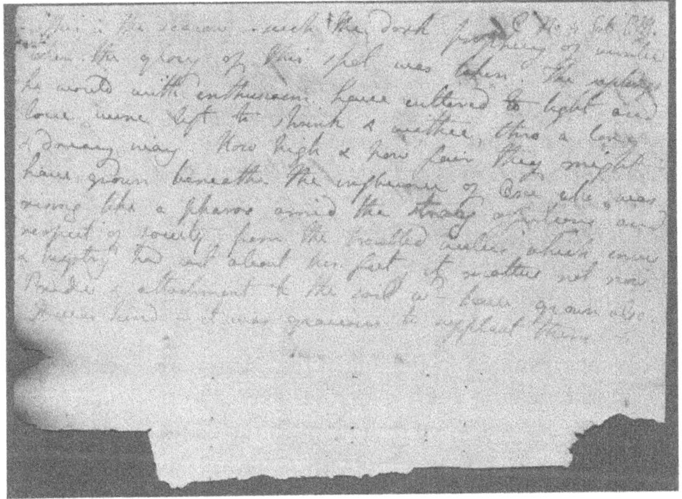

Figure 2.2 Unfolded parcel from Mary Moody Emerson Almanack, 1826. Emerson family papers, 1699–1939. MS Am 1280.235 (385, folders 1–17). Ralph Waldo Emerson Memorial Association deposit, Houghton Library, Harvard University, Cambridge, MA

up new levels of textual analysis that are enhanced by the reader's ability to touch the manuscript.

Reading diary manuscripts encourages an awareness of the unusual but powerful modes of self-expression that paper documents contain, and which may only be visible or legible to a person holding the text in their hands. But learning how to interpret the visual and tactile aspects of a manuscript requires a specialized skill set, which Evyn Kropf defines as "material manuscript literacy" (70). The following questions help readers to develop their material manuscript literacy. By fostering a detailed awareness of the material characteristics of a diary manuscript, readers are equipped to draw conclusions that will supplement readings of the text that focus on the diary's contents or on relevant contextual issues such as the diarist's biography or the historical period.

- What material format or medium does the diarist employ? Why do you think this medium is employed?
- Is the diary bound or unbound? What are the implications for how the diary can or should be read?
- Is the diary handmade or manufactured? What might this reveal about the diarist?
- How does the medium dictate, or seek to dictate, the content of the diary?
- Does the diarist conform to or diverge from the dictates of the medium?
- What kind, quality, texture, or size is the paper? What does this reveal?
- What writing instrument does the diarist use? How does this impact the text and/or its readability? Do shades of ink or pencil indicate when or how often the diarist wrote?
- Characterize the diarist's handwriting. Are there any significant patterns or changes in their writing? Are these related to the diary's contents?
- Are there any other significant visual patterns within the diary? What do they communicate?
- How does the diarist use the space of the page? Is there unused white space? Does the diarist maintain or write within marginal space?

- How and where does the diarist record dates or other temporal markers?
- Is chronological time employed to structure the text or does it follow another organizational logic?
- Does the diarist incorporate visual images or materials within the text (clippings, illustrations, drawings, photographs, etc.)? Do these relate to the diary's contents? If so, how?
- Does the diarist incorporate other modes of record-keeping such as debts or expenses, book lists, important dates, etc.? Where and how are these included? What does this indicate about the diary's function?
- Does the diarist use a code or other visual symbols, including abbreviations or initials? What is their function?
- Is there any evidence of concealment strategies such as omissions, erasures, or excisions? Is it possible to deduce who did it? When? Why?
- Is there any evidence that the diarist anticipated or sought a reading audience? How does that impact your analysis of the text?
- Does the material text indicate that the diary was read? Does this evidence appear as editorial intervention, insertion, commentary, censorship, or in some other form?
- If you are reading more than one manuscript diary by the same individual, are their material practices the same or different across multiple volumes? What is the significance of the diarist's consistency or variation?
- What information is available regarding the manuscript's history? Who preserved it, and why? How did it come to be held in a particular archive? What does this context indicate about the diary itself?

Facsimile Editions

Facsimile editions of diaries are print editions of diary manuscripts that do not transcribe, analyze, or annotate the original. Instead, they present a straightforward photographic reproduction of the text. Their straightforward quality has often led facsimiles to be dismissed as simplistic and unrigorous modes of reproduction, lacking the theoretical complexity of other editions. Scholars like Dino Buzzetti and Jerome McGann have challenged this notion and underlined the complex, interpretive demands that producing a facsimile involves (para. 5). As George Bornstein writes, facsimiles are not replicas but "new editions" in and of themselves (101). As such, they mediate the reader's access to the original, shaping in subtle but important ways how the reader interprets the text. Many modern facsimile editions, lavishly illustrated with color photographs, have more in common with collectible art or gift books than with conventional reading editions. The rise in digitization technology has resulted in a concomitant decline in the production of facsimile editions because it can be more cost effective to digitize a visually complex manuscript than to print a facsimile. Yet, several significant facsimile editions are worth acknowledging, such as those of the diaries and notebooks kept by Jean-Michel Basquiat (American, 1960–1988), Kurt Cobain (American, 1967–1994), and Frida Kahlo (Mexican, 1907–1954), as well as collections of illustrated diaries such as Lejeune and Bogaert's *Un Journal à Soi* and Snyder's *Beyond Words*.

- What about the diary or the diarist made the text a candidate for a facsimile edition? Who is the intended audience and how does this shape the editorial choices made in reproducing the text?
- In what ways does the facsimile edition differ from the original manuscript in terms of size, color, texture, length, content, etc.? How do these differences impact your interpretation of the text?
- What additional information about the diary would be useful to develop a full understanding of the text?

Self-Edited Editions

Self-edited editions are diaries that have been edited by their authors, including both manuscript and published editions. Diarists edit their diaries for a variety of reasons: for their own purposes, in anticipation of future readers, or to prepare the text for publication. First-stage editing can take many forms such as adding marginal comments or annotations to previous diary entries from a later perspective, inserting clarifying information, decrypting codes, and so forth. Very often, diarists edit their diaries to conceal information they once recorded by crossing out text, removing pages, or the like. These changes may be made directly to the paper manuscript, leaving traces on the document that can provide a roadmap of the diarist's alterations. However, it can sometimes be challenging to definitively conclude whether the alterations to a diary manuscript were made by the diarist or by someone else, whose motives for editing the text would be their own. Therefore, readers must be careful when drawing conclusions about the significance of editorial changes to a diary manuscript.

Some diarists edit their diaries for publication, a practice that challenges the idea that diarists write only for themselves. The intention to publish is one that exposes diarists to intense criticism, even by other diarists. Virginia Woolf stated, "a diary written to be published in the author's lifetime is no better than a private version of the newspaper, and often worse" ("John" 259). Woolf's criticism sums up the belief that diaries written for publication will be superficial and insincere rather than intimate and honest. If the intention to publish exposes diarists to scorn, so too does the act of editing a diary for publication. Anaïs Nin (American, 1903–1977) began publishing her diaries during her lifetime but after her death, new editions of her diaries were published. These "unexpurgated" diaries are markedly different from the ones Nin published and demonstrate the extent of the changes she made to produce the earlier, self-edited editions. These changes include not only sentence-level revisions and rearrangement of entries, but also the erasure of key characters like Nin's husband, who is absent from the self-edited editions. Changes like these only become evident when multiple versions of the diary are available to be compared, although it is important to note that, in Nin's case, the original handwritten manuscripts are not easily accessible (they are in an archive at the University of California Los Angeles) and the unexpurgated editions are themselves edited and abridged. Many readers found the fact that Nin edited her diary so significantly to be unforgivable. As Katha Pollitt wrote,

> we were led to believe that the first series of diaries constituted an amazingly veracious document, in which a woman laid bare her inner life … [n]ow we are asked to accept [the unexpurgated editions] on the same grounds, although in important respects they falsify the earlier volumes.
>
> (BR3)

Other readers have concluded that Nin's self-edited diaries should be classified as works of autobiography, not diary, because they lack the spontaneous and un-crafted quality believed to define the diary. Alternately, Nin's editorial practices can themselves be analyzed as modes of self-expression. Comparing Nin's self-edited editions against the unexpurgated editions sheds light on Nin's conception of herself, her authorial goals, and her understanding of the diary genre.

Self-edited diary editions call into question several preconceptions about the diary: That diarists write for themselves alone and do not want or seek a reading audience, and that diaries are artless, immediate, and unliterary forms of writing, distinct in quality and style from autobiographical genres that are intended to be published. Self-edited diaries reveal that some writers do conceive of the diary as a publishable form of literature, and engage in acts of composition, revision, and editing that are identical to those authors perform when writing conventional literary texts. Moreover, self-edited editions throw into flux the perception of diary manuscripts as truth and published texts as fictions. When reading diaries prepared for publication by their authors, readers will find it productive to think of editorial revisions as forms of authorship that add layers of meaning to the diary's contents.

- What information is available regarding how, why, or when the diarist edited the text?
- Is it possible to compare the self-edited edition against the diary manuscript and/or other editions? If yes, what changes

did the diarist make and what do they reveal? If no, how does this fact impact your reading of the self-edited edition?

- How does the diarist address, explicitly or implicitly, the critique that diarists who seek publication are not presenting an authentic version of themselves? How does this perception shape your own interpretation of the text?

Family-Edited Editions

Family-edited diaries are diaries that have been edited by people close to the diarist: spouses, parents, children, descendants, friends, heirs, and so forth. These editorial changes may be made in addition to the diarist's own edits or they may be the only alterations to the text. Family editions are notorious for their efforts to protect or enhance the reputation of the diarist. Relatives and descendants are often deeply invested in promoting an idealized version of their relative, a motive that drives some to extreme acts of textual mutilation including omitting what they see as embarrassing or explicit content. As mentioned earlier, when readers encounter such alterations to a manuscript diary, they may not be able to definitively identify who made the changes, which complicates the work of understanding why the changes were made or what they mean. It may be possible to gain greater clarity about these issues when reading diaries prepared for publication by family members. Family-edited editions reflect not only the diarist's values or contexts, but those of their family members – and there are times when these are in conflict. For example, when the niece of Jeb Alexander [a.k.a. Carter Newman Bealer] (American, 1899–1965) published his diaries in 1993, she created a pseudonym to hide his identity due to his frank account of his homosexuality. Although popular attitudes toward homosexuality were less restrictive in the 1990s than in Alexander's own lifetime, they nevertheless shaped the published text, demonstrating how family-edited editions may need to be situated within multiple historical contexts. Alexander's niece's changes to the text also display how nonprofessional editors employ editorial techniques unlikely to be used by academic or professional editors. For instance, she condenses Alexander's five siblings into one brother because "I think the reader would have found it tiresome to keep track of them" (4). As we will see, critical editions edited by academic editors follow rigorous rules regarding the accurate representation of the text, but family editions are not held to these standards and, as a result, are often more concerned with story than with historical accuracy. As Dan Doll argues, many family editors are engaged foremost in building a monument to their ancestor, rather than in providing readers with a comprehensive reading edition (217).

The history of Anne Frank's diary demonstrates how family-edited diaries can raise difficult questions about authorship, ownership, copyright, and profit. The history of the composition, editing, and publication of Frank's diary has received extensive attention, particularly since a 1986 critical edition of the diary reconstructed three versions of the diary: the A version, Frank's first draft; the B version, Frank's self-edited draft; and the C version, the edition composed by Otto Frank, Anne's father, which combined parts of A, B, and other fragments of Anne's writing. Although many readers are fascinated by Frank's self-editing practices, it was Otto Frank's role in the production of the earliest print editions of the diary that classifies them as family editions. Like other family editors, Otto omitted portions of Anne's diary that cast her in a negative light, such as her bitter complaints about those with whom she was in hiding. The 1986 critical edition allows readers to read the three versions of the diary in side-by-side columns, demonstrating the extent of Otto's alterations and appearing to restore Anne's original voice (Prose; Shandler). But, the controversy did not end there. Most print editions of Frank's diary identify Otto Frank as the text's editor but in 2015 a new question emerged regarding whether Otto should instead be considered a coauthor, given the extensive role he played in crafting the published diary. The Swiss foundation Anne Frank Fonds, which holds the diary's copyright, put forth this idea in an effort to maintain control over the text. According to European law, copyright expires seventy years after the death of the author, meaning that Frank's diary would enter the public domain on January 1, 2016. But if Otto were recognized as a coauthor, the European copyright would be extended until 2050. (The diary remains under copyright in the United States until 2047.) At the time of this writing, Otto's status as coauthor remains in dispute but the question itself reveals how the diary's authorship is shaped both by its composition/editorial history and by its worldwide reception (Carvajal; Moody). Anne Frank's diary teaches us that family-edited editions are influenced by interpersonal relationships, by the desire for familial legacy, by a need to protect or craft a diarist's reputation, by legal concerns regarding copyright and ownership, and by profit – creating a multilayered framework that shapes how readers encounter and interpret the text.

- What information is available about the editorial changes made by family members or other close relations? What personal motives or societal values are reflected in these changes?
- In what ways can you distinguish between the diarist's goals for their self-presentation and the editor's goals regarding the public perception of the diarist?
- What can family editions teach us about the role of love, care, protection, or promotion in the work of editing diaries?

Mediated Editions

In literary studies, scholars are attentive to the fact that when someone other than the author plays a significant role in publishing a text, that individual can take on a mediating function – in effect, standing between the reader and the original text. The impact of the mediator can be exacerbated by issues of gender, race, or class, particularly if the mediator is a member of a privileged class and the author is not. For example, in the past, white editors were often involved in publishing the life narratives of black writers. For many readers of the time, having the white editor's endorsement legitimated the text. For contemporary readers, however, the role of white editors of black-authored texts raises questions about the authenticity of the text as a representation of the black experience. Is it possible to recover black voices when white editors have shaped the text for their own purposes? Similar dynamics may be at work in male-edited but female-authored texts, and so forth. When the editor inhabits a position of privilege and the author is dependent upon the editor for their access to publication, a power differential is established that can have implications for what is written or how it is written. Scholars have interpreted this dynamic in many ways: as a form of silencing, as cultural appropriation, as a negotiation, as a dialogue, and even as a form of collaboration or coauthorship. Informed readers will not take mediated editions at face value but instead interrogate the ways in which the author is framed within a lens of power and privilege.

The diaries of Carolina Maria de Jesus (Brazilian, 1914–1977) exemplify the challenges of reading meditated diaries. De Jesus was a black woman who resided in the *favelas* (slums) of São Paulo and who supported herself and her children by sorting through trash. The journalist Audálio Dantas discovered that de Jesus had written a diary and began publishing it in 1958, first as a newspaper column and then in book form. The diary was a worldwide sensation because it gave readers a glimpse into the life of a woman who was triply marginalized due to her race, class, and gender. However, some readers questioned whether de Jesus had the ability to write the diary and speculated that Dantas was the real author. Others criticized Dantas's role in controlling access to the diary and profiting from its publication. The publication in 1999 of unedited portions of de Jesus's diary proved that Dantas had edited the text, primarily by deleting diary entries in which de Jesus expressed bitterness toward the Brazilian upper class (Levine and Meihy 15). Although the original diary manuscript remains in Dantas's private possession, the unexpurgated edition gives readers access to the editorial, publication, and reception history of the diary in order to examine the role of bias in the production of the text. Reading mediated editions of diaries calls for a careful consideration of how the production of a publishable text may involve more than editing the text for readability. It may also involve locating a diarist within societal systems that are inherently discriminatory toward the diarist and therefore limit what they can say or how they will be received.

- Identify the structural differences between the author and editor that make the edition a mediated edition. Why was a mediating editor considered necessary for producing the edition?
- How and why did the editor change the text? In what ways is the editor's own voice or perspective present within the text?
- Which, if any, of the following theories of mediation appears most useful for interpreting the edition and the relationship between the diarist and editor: silencing, cultural appropriation, negotiation, dialogue, collaboration, or coauthorship? Why?

Critical Editions

Critical editions of diaries are those that have been carefully edited by scholars knowledgeable about editorial practices and about the historical or literary contexts that inform the original text. Critical editions are generally designed to make a text accessible to a reading audience that might not have the opportunity to access the original or the expertise to interpret it without assistance. Historically, critical editions were published books but digital critical editions are becoming more common and take advantage of the multimedia and collaborative affordances of digital media. Whether print or digital, critical editions are situated within the scholarly field of textual editing, which has its own complex history, ongoing theoretical debates, and shifting guidelines regarding best practices. For the most part, critical editions are:

Edited: Decisions are made by an editor or editorial team about which text or which part(s) of a text to reproduce, and how to reproduce it.

Transcribed: The original text, whether a handwritten manuscript or previously published edition, is rendered in a standardized print format.

Annotated: Information considered useful to readers is provided, usually in the form of endnotes, footnotes, or hypertext links.

Introduced and contextualized: Essays or supplementary materials like maps, family trees, or glossaries situate the text within its historical or literary context.

Peer reviewed: The text is evaluated by other scholars regarding its fulfillment of editorial standards.

Paul Eggert argues that readers of critical editions can learn to discern the principles that underlie the editor's decision-making by studying the edition's "architecture and interface," or what is known as the editorial apparatus (98). For this reason, reading a critical edition of a diary should start with an investigation of the editor's choices and how they have determined the edition's contents. As Dan Doll states, behind every editorial choice about how to present a diary to readers is an idea about "what a diary is" and what the editor "believes a reader reads a diary for or what readers should read a diary for" (213). Understanding those choices will better prepare the reader to interpret the diary itself.

Critical editions are often granted the status of authoritative texts. They present what comes to be accepted as the best, most accurate, or most trustworthy version of the original text. Yet, the authoritative nature of the edition also deserves to be examined because it can, at times, lead readers to discount the subjective or political nature of editorial work. As an archival practice, editing is bound up within the politics of the archive discussed at the start of this chapter. Equally, editors are the products of their times and their choices regarding which texts to edit and how the edition will be presented can be shaped by their values, contexts, or political views. Michelle R. Warren makes a compelling case for the role that politics plays in determining which texts get edited, reprinted, disseminated, and studied (124). Certainly it is no accident that most critical editions are devoted to canonical works or authors, or function to secure canonical status for a work or author. Nontraditional materials, marginalized authors, or works that deal with controversial subjects are less likely to be granted the institutional status of a critical edition. Besides literary hierarchies, we can link an edition's politics to professional hierarchies and labor conditions within the academy, begging questions like: Who does this work, how it is funded, and what institutions support, own, or profit from the results? While we may not be accustomed to thinking about editing or book design through the prism of power, it can be worthwhile to explore these dimensions of a critical edition.

The critical and popular editions of Ralph Waldo Emerson's diaries provide a roadmap for considering the debates that can surround critical editions, particularly regarding their claim to authoritative status. Emerson (American, 1803–1882) was a philosopher and writer who left behind over 200 unpublished journals, notebooks, pocket diaries, and memoranda. Emerson's son and grandson edited the first print edition of his journals between 1906 and 1914, an edition that exemplifies the function of family-edited diaries as monuments to the diarist's memory. These editors excised Emerson's references to anger, fear, humor, and sex to sanitize their subject and thereby to promote his reputation – and by extension, the editors' own, as his decendents (Porte vii).

In the 1950s, an editorial team lead by William H. Gilman undertook a new critical edition of Emerson's journals that they explicitly positioned against its predecessor. The sixteen volume Gilman edition, published from 1960 to 1982, set out to present a fuller, less idealized portrait by replicating as accurately as possible the contents of what the editors called Emerson's "raw journals" (xxxii). The goal of scrupulous textual accuracy led the editors to develop a complex transcription system using diacritical marks such as <> and | to represent the messy, informal features of Emerson's handwritten manuscripts. This editorial choice displayed the editor's belief that every detail of Emerson's writing, even his misspellings, insertions, cross outs, and erasures, deserved to be presented to readers. However the fact that this choice privileged comprehensiveness over readability made the edition subject to extensive criticism. In a scathing review, Louis Mumford stated that the "standard of exactitude in transcription" employed by the editors results in "ruthless typographical mutilation" (4), which he illustrated by quoting the following sentence:

> The best visions of the Christian <are> ↑ correspond ↓ cold ↑ ly ↓ & imperfect ↑ ly ↓ to the promise of infinite reward<s> which the scripture | contains | reveals |.
>
> (Emerson I.193)

According to Mumford, reading Emerson's writing in this form is like peering through barbed wire, as the transcription mechanism stands between the reader and the text instead of facilitating access (4). For Mumford, this edition does not give readers access to the true Emerson but isolates him further by making his journals accessible only to scholars equipped with the skills to sort through arcane textual details. Critiques like these show that every choice editors make – down to their choice of punctuation – can be analyzed for what they reveal about the editor's goals for the text or beliefs about their readers.

The history of the publication of Emerson's diaries also points to the need to consider how critical editions might participate in shoring up literary hierarchies. The fact that there have been three major print editions of Emerson's diaries published since 1960, as well as editions of his poetry journal and topical notebooks, indicates that institutional support for Emerson's literary legacy remains ongoing. Compare this to a general lack of funding or publication opportunities for editorial projects on noncanonical writers, whose diaries remain inaccessible to both scholars and general readers. In other words, because critical editions confer institutional or canonical status, they can be designed to elevate previously marginalized or under-studied figures, or to reinforce well-established standing within academic circles.

Considering the goals of a critical edition, even those that are unstated, will help to elucidate the arguments that the text as a whole makes. The questions below foreground the fact that, although the editorial apparatus establishes a lens through which to read the diary manuscript, the lens itself is not a neutral device but a mechanism for making a critical argument about the text.

- Where has the editor placed information about the medium, form, or structure of the original manuscript? How does this choice impact the reading experience?
- If the edition involves the abridgment or partial reproduction of the original manuscript, what principles governed these choices?
- What protocols or guidelines were employed regarding the transcription of the manuscript text?
- Has the editor standardized the text? (For example, correcting misspellings, adding punctuation, etc.) Why or why not?
- How does the editor communicate the author's own editing or alteration of the original text (revision, correction, excision, concealment, etc.)?
- What information about the original manuscript is most important to bear in mind as you read the critical edition of the diary?
- What contextual information does the editor provide that is most useful for interpreting the text?
- What supplemental information does the edition provide? (For example, chronology, family tree, glossary, maps, etc.)
- How has the editor organized the text and how does this mirror or alter the diary's original organization?
- How does the editor characterize their relationship to the diary/diarist, and how does this impact their choices?
- When was the critical edition produced, and how might the historical context have influenced the editor's choices?
- How does the edition situate the diary and its author within relevant literary contexts? What argument does the edition make about the status of the author or text within literary history?

Digitized Editions

Digitized editions are editions of original materials (sometimes manuscripts but also previously printed materials) that have been digitally reproduced and made available online. In this context, it is important to distinguish between *digitized diaries* and *digital diaries*, the latter of which are diaries authored through digital software or online media and which are the focus of Chapter 5. Digitized diaries are manuscript or print diaries that have been digitized by individuals other than their authors, usually archivists, editors, or academics. In recent years, a large number of diaries have been digitized and are now accessible through open-access websites. The implications are significant: Not only will the increase of digitized diaries make it possible to analyze a broader range of texts, digital reproductive technology enables readers to explore the material features of manuscripts in new and innovative ways – and without the necessity of travel to an archive. However, digital humanities scholars are quick to remind readers that although digitized materials or digital surrogates may look very much like the original source, they are not. As Bob Nicholson states, "[digitization] creates something new; sources are 'remediated' and not just reproduced. Though a digitized text may look familiar, it is not the same source; we are able to access, read, organize, and analyze it in radical new ways" (64). Digital literacy requires thinking critically about the changes that digitization makes to previously analog texts.

Resource: For a list of digitized diaries, visit Henderson's *Diary Index*, www.diaryindex.com.

One of the most important contributions digitization makes to the study of diary manuscripts is that it grants readers access to the visual features of the original text, making the privileged experience of reading a manuscript in an archive available to a larger number of people. It is now possible to look closely at a manuscript diary online, to zoom in on the unusual characteristics of the text, and draw conclusions based on this information, applying many of the same analytical questions I outlined above for the "in person" study of manuscript diaries. In fact, Kropf argues that material manuscript literacy is an invaluable prerequisite for working with digital surrogates, as readers will be better able to discern what textual information is gained and what is lost when accessing a manuscript in digital form (56). For instance, some digital interfaces will enable readers to manipulate the text in ways that might not be possible with an actual manuscript: to enhance color or resolution, rotate or alter scale, or magnify. This is in addition to groundbreaking research tools such as the capacity to conduct keyword searches or to save discoveries through bookmark, screenshot, or download – tools either not available or not as easily implemented with material texts. And, once diaries are digitized, the transcribed texts and their metadata can be analyzed through text mining, data visualization, geospatial mapping, or other digital humanities tools. Yet, it also remains true that digitization may restrict information about the manuscript, primarily because it utilizes a visual medium and excludes other senses such as touch, taste, sound, and smell, which some insist are crucial to interpreting a manuscript. Not only do digitized texts focus on the visual, they tend to limit their reproduction to two-dimensional, book-like formats despite the fact that digital technologies make a variety of formats possible (Gabler 48). One expression of this continued privileging of print formats is that many digitized diaries require readers to painstakingly page forward and backward in order to navigate the text as if they were holding a codex or book in their hands, when the digital medium should allow readers to enter, explore, or even remix the text in innovative ways.

Another positive achievement of diary digitization is that it enables a more diverse range of diaries to come to light. As discussed above, critical editions of diaries have tended to reproduce the writing of famous or canonical authors. Digitized diaries promise to help break down these hierarchies. Examples of this diversification can already be seen in online repositories such as

Brunel University's *Burnett Archive of Working Class Autobiographies* and the University of California's *Japanese American Relocation Digital Archives*. Digitized diaries will also help to break down national boundaries, facilitating a global perspective on the genre and its history. No longer limited to working in locally accessible archives, readers have the opportunity to generate a new body of knowledge about how diaries were written in different times and places, and by people whose voices have often been historically erased. Digital technology also enables readers to take an active role in the production of this material. Editions produced through collaboration and public involvement, called "social editions," employ online interactivity to harness the collective wisdom and labor of interested individuals across the globe, colloquially known as "volunpeers" (Siemens; Ferriter). The diary archive has already begun to benefit from these efforts, notably through projects like the Smithsonian Institution's *Transcription Center*, which facilitates the collective transcription of numerous diary manuscripts in its archive, and *Operation War Diary*, a public effort to annotate the British National Archive's collection of World War I diaries.

Two digitized diaries exemplify the ways that digitization technologies are opening up the diary archive. *Memorable Days: The Emilie Davis Diaries* digitizes the pocket diaries kept by an African American woman during the U.S. Civil War. Davis's diaries provide us with a rare glimpse into the life of a free woman of color at a moment in history when debates over race, rights, and citizenship divided the country. *Memorable Days* gives readers access to Davis's handwritten diary manuscripts, as well as to transcribed versions of these materials that are helpfully annotated with information regarding the historical period. The digitized manuscript makes it possible for readers to appreciate how Davis creatively used the limited space of her palm-sized pocket diaries to record the aspects of her life she deemed most significant: her social life, romantic interests, and educational endeavors. *Livingstone's 1871 Field Diary* digitizes the diary written by David Livingstone, the British explorer, during an expedition to the Congo. Livingstone originally wrote his diary on newspaper print, writing crossways over the printed text, using ink that he made himself. The ink had faded so significantly that the diary was essentially unreadable until spectral imaging technology was employed to reveal the contents. In this instance, digitization was instrumental in rendering the text in a readable form. The *Field Diary* edition presents the diary along with substantial supporting materials including essays on the manuscript, the spectral imaging process, and Livingstone's life and legacy. These websites exemplify what digitization makes possible by enabling readers to engage with complex and historically significant diary manuscripts through an online medium.

Both *Memorial Days* and *Livingstone's 1871 Field Diary* can be considered digital critical editions. Like the print critical editions discussed above, online resources of this kind fulfill the expectation of informed editorial practices and substantially researched scholarly contexts. However, most digitized diaries do not benefit from such robust framing. Instead, they are simply digitized (scanned and posted online) with minimal additional information. Many do not provide even the most basic supporting materials such as biographical data, textual history, or print transcription. Unlike critical editions, which provide an editorial apparatus to support and enhance the reading experience, these spare editions place the burden upon readers to decipher texts and locate them within a historical context. In addition, in many instances, the supporting materials and research tools that are provided are flawed, including inaccurate transcriptions, unreliable search capabilities, and poorly executed metadata. These issues indicate how digitization is not a simple solution to the challenges of archival access but may present a new set of challenges. We should explore such sites with a critical eye, taking advantage of what is useful but aware of what may be problematic.

In sum, digitized materials are not identical to manuscript originals and the digital format may either enhance or limit an interpretation of the text, creating a unique reading experience. Students and scholars bear a particular responsibility to acknowledge when they have worked with a digital surrogate, a citation practice that recognizes the fundamental differences between manuscript and digitized editions of the same text. Digitized editions represent a growing area within diary studies, with the potential to radically reshape our understanding of the genre, but readers need to approach them critically and with an awareness of the ways in which the digital format influences the reading and interpretative experience.

- If the digitized diary provides access to a visual reproduction of the manuscript original, the reading questions for Manuscript Diaries can be applied.
- If the digitized diary is a digital critical edition, the reading questions for Critical Editions can be applied.
- Does the digital platform indicate why the diary was digitized? If so, why? If not, what do you posit as a reason?
- Who made the digitized edition (individuals or institutions)? Who hosts the online text interface? What does this reveal about the text?
- What supplementary materials or interpretative tools does the digital interface provide? How do these impact your reading?
- What challenges does the digital interface present, if any? How can you overcome or address these challenges?
- Is a print transcription of the manuscript original provided? Is it accurate?
- What aspects of the material text are not available to readers in the digital format? How does this impact your understanding of the text?
- How is the editorial apparatus (if any) presented? How does this information shape your understanding of the text?
- Is there any mechanism provided for readers to participate in this digitization project? What kinds of public participation are invited, and why?
- How does the fact that this digitized edition is accessed online shape your perception of the diary, or of diary writing in general?

Making New Editions

This chapter provides readers with interpretative frameworks for exploring diaries in a variety of forms from handwritten manuscripts, to edited print editions, to digitized editions. I conclude by proposing that readers consider the ways they could participate in making new editions of diaries that have not yet been recovered but which deserve to be made accessible to the reading public. There are a variety of ways that readers can make new editions. They can write an introduction to an unknown or little-studied diary that would make the text more comprehensible to other readers. They can transcribe a handwritten diary, even organizing or participating in a transcribathon to harness the collective effort of multiple volunteers. They can digitize a diary, learning from existing digitized diary editions about best practices for making diaries legible through online platforms. Any of these projects could be taken on individually, in working groups, or in partnership with academic institutions or archives – including archives that hold specific diary manuscripts. The materials generated could be deposited in archives alongside diary manuscripts, published in academic or popular journals, or posted online through a host of open-access platforms. As digital tools continue to change and improve, new modes of access, engagement, and dissemination will become available, giving readers more and better ways to create new editions.

Contributing to a diary edition is one of the most powerful ways of reading a diary. As we've seen, making editorial choices about how to transform a diary requires a deep engagement with the text, as well as with the ethics, politics, and mechanics of textual preservation, reproduction, and circulation. Diary editors are active participants in the production of the text, developing a level of knowledge and expertise that most readers cannot match. Yet, as the previous discussion of diary editions indicated, there are many different ways of editing diaries, each with their own strengths and weaknesses. Be responsible and ethical. Be creative and break new ground. Find what works best for the diary or diarist, your community, or the wider public, and for your own social, political, or intellectual goals.

Essential Question #2: Is the Diary a Feminine Genre?

It is a common perception that diaries are a feminine form of writing, more likely to be undertaken by girls or women than by boys or men. And, because patriarchal culture disparages femininity, the association between women and diaries has contributed to the dismissal of the genre both by academics and the general public. But scholars generally agree that the genre is not inherently feminine but rather *feminized*, a historical process that constructs a gendered character for the diary and its authors.

These issues are related to the *gender paradox* within the literary history of the diary, which can be summarized as follows: The most celebrated and canonical diaries are those written by men but the genre as a whole is characterized as feminine. Standard histories of the genre center on influential diaries by male writers such as Samuel Pepys, James Boswell, Henry David Thoreau, Henri-Frédéric Amiel, the Goncourt brothers, André Gide, and so forth. These diarists are credited with either establishing the conventions of the genre or perfecting its aesthetic qualities. Yet, at the same time, the diary is overwhelmingly perceived as a feminine form of writing, an attribute utilized to devalue the diary as a literary form. Many feminist critics have remarked upon the contradiction inherent to these ideas. How can the absence of women from the mainstream history of the genre be reconciled with the pervasive idea that the genre is inherently feminine? Why are men credited with creating the conventions of the genre, yet women are thought to more easily and naturally take up those conventions?

For many scholars, the perception of the diary as feminine opens up an opportunity to rewrite the standard history of the genre, as well as to challenge the pejorative characterization of femininity. As discussed in Chapter 1, diary historians recognize that women's diary writing was widespread both before and after male diarists gained prominence through publication and critical acclaim. The standard history of the diary reflects the gender bias of early critics who considered women's accounts of their domestic or interior lives to lack significance. As Elizabeth Hampsten writes, "How many times has someone said that writings of a particular woman had no historical value because they were merely about daily events?" (xi). However, women's contributions to the diary have gained new appreciation due to the work of feminist scholars who have recovered and championed women's diaries. This effort corresponds with an equally important project of restoring value to the feminine. Resisting the idea that accounts of women's lives are trivial or self-indulgent, scholars instead assert that women's life writing testifies to the multifaceted, beautiful, and vital nature of the female and feminine.

One popular argument by feminist scholars is that the diary is uniquely qualified to meet the needs of women writers. Historically denied access to opportunities for public speech, including publication, diaries provided women with a literary outlet. In fact, the perception of the diary as a private genre gave women an alibi should they be accused of violating gender norms by writing. Elizabeth Podnieks states that women could "find in its private, unassuming pages a place to express themselves, confirm their value, and paradoxically comply with and challenge the silence prescribed for respectable female conduct" (46). Scholars also note that the structure of the diary is particularly compatible with the patterns of women's daily lives: "emotional, fragmentary, interrupted, modest, not to be taken seriously, private, restricted, daily, trivial, formless, concerned with the self, as endless as their tasks" (Moffat 5). Women could incorporate diary writing into a day already broken up by repetitive chores and responsibilities. Indeed, the format of daily diary entries both echoes and elevates the cyclical nature of domestic life. Striking evidence of this fact can be found in women's use of the diary to track their menstrual cycles, sexual experiences, birth control, pregnancies, and menopause. In the past, such matters were often rendered in veiled language or through visual codes. Emily Hawley Gillespie (American, 1838–1888) recorded sex with her husband with three exclamation marks in the margin of her diary (185) and Annie Ray (American, 1855–1931) indicated the start of her menstrual cycle with a star and sex with her husband with a flower (120). Nor were women alone in recognizing the value of the diary as a record of women's bodily cycles. As Sara Crangle has shown, Leonard Woolf (British, 1880–1969) kept a detailed account of his wife Virginia Woolf's menstrual cycles and menopause in his own diaries. Examples such as these indicate the particular uses diaries played in women's lives, furthering the idea that the genre is uniquely designed to represent their experiences.

However, feminist critics are aware that this argument runs the risk of affirming an essentialist notion of gender. The parallels between female embodied experience and the diary form described above may appear to suggest that women have an innate or natural association with the genre – a position that contemporary scholars resoundingly reject. Rebecca Hogan states, "it is possible to see how we may describe a writing strategy or literary form as 'feminine' or 'masculine' regardless of the sex of its practitioner or author" (95). Instead, it is worthwhile to consider how that writing strategy or literary form became seen as feminine or masculine, and why such gendering persists. Rebecca Steinitz specifies that diary studies should "take gender as an object of inquiry rather than a given" (6). To accomplish this goal, scholars explore the *feminization* of the genre: the processes through which the genre became associated with femininity, regardless of who was writing or what they were writing about. For the most part, scholars believe that this historical process occurred during the nineteenth century, long after the genre originated. For instance, Jane H. Hunter shows that nineteenth-century children's magazines popularized the idea that diary writing was an activity appropriate for girls because it could help them develop a submissive and self-effacing identity (55–58). These and other nineteenth-century texts linked diary characteristics (privacy, self-scrutiny, order, refinement) to a "naturally" feminine self and used the genre to socialize children into a male/female gender binary. While the consequences may be most acute for female-identified individuals, male-identified diarists also pay the price when diary writing is perceived as an effeminate activity and therefore subject to misogynistic and homophobic stigmas. However, although the feminization of the diary and diarists is pervasive, this phenomenon does not prevent diarists from using their diaries to represent non-binary gender identities. The diary accommodates the life narratives of cisgender, transgender, and gender non-conforming individuals – as well as those by people across the sexuality spectrum – which makes the genre an invaluable repository for stories about how gender and sexuality norms are created and internalized, and how individuals resist or revise these norms.

Do more women write diaries than men? It is a question that is almost impossible to answer. The historical record is notoriously unreliable, particularly given the likelihood that women's private writings were not saved or archived. If the records of the past are not helpful, neither are contemporary practices. Once the diary became viewed as feminine, this perspective created a self-perpetuating phenomenon. By the early twentieth century, pink diaries were being marketed to girls, reinforcing the idea that diary writing was an inherently female activity, particularly appropriate for adolescent girls. Yet, there is ample evidence that many diarists persisted in their writing regardless of whether they conformed to this narrow category.

Is the diary a feminine genre? It would be more accurate to say that the diary is a feminized genre and to pose alternate questions: How does this gendering occur? What patriarchal ideas does it reinforce? How does the perception of the diary as feminine impact the style or content of individual diaries? How is the diary employed by diarists to explore ideas about gender or sexuality, including those that challenge conventional binaries? Addressing these questions will help readers to develop a thorough understanding of the diary and its relationship to gender identity.

3 Reading the Diary as Literature

If you were describing a diary to someone completely unfamiliar with the genre, what would you say? We've already seen that some of the most common descriptors of diaries such as private or feminine are worth rethinking. In the absence of these terms, what defines the genre? Many scholars have found it productive to think of the diary in comparison to other forms of writing such as the memoir or the novel. These comparisons are frequently intended to prove that the diary is a legitimate form of literature by virtue of its similarities to these established genres. Yet this move can have the unintended consequence of placing the diary in a secondary and lesser position compared to these other forms. When the diary is judged according the standards of the memoir, novel, or other literary genres, it is often found to be lacking. Philippe Lejeune writes, "Most criticisms of the diary are based on value systems that are fundamentally at odds with the diary's value systems" (*On Diary* 153). This chapter is designed to identify the value systems that are appropriate to the diary genre so that readers can analyze diaries on their own terms.

As I argued in Chapter 1, it is worthwhile to understand why certain myths gained prominence in the popular perception of diaries, particularly considering how influential these ideas continue to be. However, the goal of this chapter is to introduce readers to a different set of characteristics or conventions that more accurately describe the genre. Understanding these conventions will prepare readers to analyze diaries as literary texts. I begin with a discussion of how attempts to define and classify the diary have shaped critical debates around the genre's place in literary studies. I then outline six characteristic genre conventions that can guide readers' engagement with diaries. I conclude by addressing common ways of misreading diaries and provide suggestions for how to avoid these missteps. Readers should complete this chapter equipped with the necessary tools to understand, interpret, and appreciate the literary characteristics of the diary.

Are Diaries Literature? Addressing the Genre Paradox

Are diaries comparable to the kinds of writing that we typically classify as literature, such as poems, plays, novels, or short stories? Do diaries reach the levels of artistic achievement, creativity, or innovation that make these works identifiably literary? Or, in looking for artistic expression in a diary, are we imposing ideals foreign to the practice of diary writing? Are diaries still diaries if they are also literature?

These questions reflect the *genre paradox* of the diary, a set of commonly held but inherently contradictory views about the genre:

- Diaries are unliterary. They are uncrafted, artless, spontaneous, and ordinary kinds of writing – and were never intended to be thought of as works of literature.
- Some diaries are literary, but primarily by distinguishing themselves from ordinary diaries. These diaries transcend their genre origins by employing recognizably literary writing styles or techniques and they deserve to be classified as literature.
- Diaries that are literary may not be authentic diaries. A diary that is too crafted, too artful, or too much like literature is subject to skepticism regarding its truthfulness and legitimacy as a work of life writing.

Each of the propositions within the genre paradox has elements of truth, yet they cannot all be true. It is important to understand these competing claims to appreciate what is at stake in the question of whether or not diaries are literature.

Many believe that diaries are not literature, especially in the sense of polished or highbrow writing. It is possible to see the diary as a genre that fulfills an important function for diarists, possesses historical value, and makes for entertaining reading, while nonetheless believing that diaries do not rise to the level of literature. Often, however, the argument that the diary is unliterary leads to dismissing the genre as a whole. For instance, William Matthews writes, "Diaries *en masse* might well be regarded as natural products, and their commonly lumpish matters and styles witness the artlessness of their writers" ("Diary as Literature" cxi). By suggesting that diaries are "natural," Matthews infers that they can be written by anyone, even by those who lack literary skills, because they require no effort, education, or sense of artistry.

Other scholars contend that while most diaries are not literary, certain ones are, a distinction that creates a hierarchy within the genre. The status of literature is usually reserved for diaries that that are descriptive, expository, or philosophical, those that employ dialog, characterization, or plot, and those that are accessible to readers. Unliterary diaries, on the other hand, are abbreviated, fragmented, or difficult to understand. These diaries are labeled "ordinary," a descriptor that has often been designed to justify the marginalization of these texts. However, in *The Extraordinary Work of Ordinary Writing*, Jennifer Sinor argues that the term "ordinary" deserves to be reclaimed within diary studies. According to Sinor, we are surrounded by ordinary forms of writing: "writing that is typically unseen or ignored … defined by its status as discardable" (5). Yet, as Sinor explains, "ordinariness" has its own complex and meaningful conventions that are worthy of analysis (187). Accordingly, to describe a diary as ordinary is not necessarily a marginalizing move but may instead be a useful descriptor for certain styles of diary writing that challenge traditional expectations regarding what counts as literature.

Sinor's argument also prompts us to consider whose diaries have been called literature, and whose have not. The "unliterary" characterization is more likely to be applied to diaries that record the lives of women, the working class, people of color, or other marginalized individuals. These writers may write in ways that oppose the formal conventions of canonical literature, perhaps because they lacked access to the literary culture and artistic traditions that define the canon. To describe their diaries as unliterary implicitly conveys a judgment upon the diarists themselves, for "[t]he tradition of devaluing ordinary writing … is equally a devaluation of the writer" (Sinor 89). Notably, the writing styles and techniques that are recognized as literary emerge out of a male-dominated tradition – and a white, Western, and elite one, as well. In this way the diary's *genre paradox* is inextricably linked to the *gender paradox* discussed in Essential Question #2.

While claiming a diary as literary may be intended to promote its status, it has the surprising effect of potentially disqualifying the text from being a diary. This is not the case with most other genres; a poem does not stop being a poem if it is characterized as literature. Yet, diaries that appear too literary can be judged to no longer be actual diaries. For readers who approach a diary with the expectation that the text will provide an unmediated record of events, the possibility that it employs literary or even fictional devices will raise concerns about its legitimacy as a diary. While claiming the diary as a form of literature is a powerful critical move, it necessitates an acknowledgment of the diary's specific relationship to truth and the expectations this creates for readers. I explore these issues in more depth in Essential Question #4.

One consequence of the debate over the diary's status as literature is that it initially drove a wedge between the diary and autobiography. Early on, when the field of autobiography studies was attempting to gain legitimacy, scholars sought to promote the literary status of autobiography and memoir, a claim made in part by distinguishing these genres from the diary. The characterization of the diary as spontaneous, nonretrospective, and fragmented was used to highlight the opposite and more admirable qualities of autobiography: reflective, retrospective, and coherent (Pascal

4–5). The distinction between the two genres was reinforced by one of the most significant theories within autobiography studies, Lejeune's "autobiographical pact." According to this theory, readers approach autobiography with an expectation that the author identified on the book's cover is identical to the protagonist/narrator of the text, fostering the book's claim to truthfulness. When he formulated this idea in the 1970s, Lejeune excluded diaries on the basis that they do not meet all the conditions that define autobiography ("Autobiographical" 4). The prominence of Lejeune's essay within autobiography studies initially contributed to the idea that the diary was not equivalent to the autobiography as a literary genre. In the decades since, both Lejeune and others have reconsidered the relevance of the autobiographical pact to diary studies, including whether or not there is a corresponding "diary pact" (Cottam 268). Today, the diary is generally perceived as one of many genres residing under the umbrella of autobiography or life writing, each with equal claim to the status of literature. Indeed, the field of autobiography studies has been instrumental in providing scholars and readers with the tools necessary to interpret and appreciate the literary character of ordinary writing.

The genre paradox has been the starting point for much diary studies scholarship and still structures many critical conversations about the diary. Scholars of the diary are well aware of the popular perception of the genre as unliterary and know that if diaries are recognized as possessing artistic or aesthetic characteristics, they can be studied, taught, and read within a literary tradition. And there remains great significance in granting recognition to writers who have historically not been considered equal participants in literary culture, but who deserve a place in literary history. Yet these moves are now made in a critical context that confers value upon a wide range of written material, including styles and forms that defy traditional standards of the literary. Accordingly, the diary can be identified as literature, placed alongside other recognizable genres like the novel or memoir, and yet be acknowledged to possess its own unique characteristics. It is within this context that the literary conventions of the diary should be interpreted and appreciated.

Reading Diary Conventions

This chapter proposes that diaries deserve to be read in ways that acknowledge and grapple with the defining features of the genre. While it remains important to contextualize diaries historically, in terms of their material form and publication histories, within the biography of the diarist, and within larger debates in literary and autobiographical studies, readers also need to be able to understand the genre's specific forms and devices. In this section, I outline six diary conventions to assist readers in interpreting the genre. Not all diaries utilize these conventions and readers will need to decide whether or not they are relevant to the diary they are reading. The absence of these conventions may be, in and of itself, a defining characteristic of the text and worth analyzing. Yet these six topics will be relevant to most diaries, as well as providing insight into some of the central issues within diary studies. Throughout I illustrate this discussion by referencing a wide range of diaries from across the globe and spanning a wide historical period in order to convey the many different and sometimes surprising ways diarists respond to these conventions.

The Diary Subject

Witold Gombrowicz (Polish, 1904–1969) famously begins his diary with these entries:

> *Monday*
> Me.
> *Tuesday*
> Me.
> *Wednesday*
> Me.
> *Thursday*
> Me.
>
> (3)

These opening entries can be thought of as simultaneously epitomizing and satirizing the self-focus of the diary. Almost all diaries employ what is known as the "autobiographical I," a first person point of view that communicates that the diarist is both writer and subject. By virtue of this use of the "I," diaries are thought to possess certain characteristics:

An individual and personal narrative voice: Diarists speak of and for themselves.
The authority of experience: Only diarists can represent their lives accurately or meaningfully.
A sense of immediacy and transparency: Diarists record events as they happen, in a direct and uncrafted way.

These characteristics create for readers an expectation of unmediated access to the diarist's life.

However, contemporary autobiographical theory contends that the "autobiographical I" is anything but a simple and straightforward representation of the author. Sidonie Smith and Julia Watson argue that the autobiographical "I" is actually four distinct "I's": The "real" or historical "I," the narrating "I," the narrated "I," and the ideological "I" (72). According to Smith and Watson, the impossibility of creating a single, unified self from these four categories reflects the complexity and historical contingency of each person. Recognizing the multi-layered nature of the textual self teaches us to pay attention to those moments when fragmentation or multiplicity becomes evident. Diaries present many such moments. For instance, Henry David Thoreau declared, "Say's I to my-self should be the motto of my Journal" (November 11, 1851). At first glance, this appears to be a quintessential statement of the diarist's purpose: to write privately about oneself and for oneself. But, read more carefully, Thoreau's distinction between "I" and "my-self" and, in particular, his unusual choice to hyphenate "myself," point to the complicated relationship between the diarist and their written self (Neufeldt 115). While we might expect the "I" of a diary to function as a direct representation of the author, Thoreau's statement instead encourages us to see that diary writing reflects the fragmentary nature of authorial perspective.

Some diarists self-consciously play with the expectation of the individualistic diary subject. For example, Emilio Renzi [a.k.a. Ricardo Piglia] (Argentine, 1941–2017) switches back and forth between first and third person throughout his diary, and imagines using multiple diaries to reflect his multiple selves. He writes,

> I am worried about my tendency to speak about myself as though I were divided, were two people … I thought I would have to keep two separate notebooks, A and B. A would contain the events, the incidents, and B the secret thoughts, the silent voice.
>
> (July 10, 1963)

A similar fantasy of two diaries appears in Anaïs Nin's diary: "I was tempted today to keep a double journal, one for things which do happen, and one for imaginary incidents which pass through my head … I live *doubly*. I'll write *doubly*" (February 3, 1928). These passages may give the impression that writing a diary creates a division within the subject by encouraging the diarist to adopt a distanced, authorial persona. Literary critics argue the contrary, stating that the diary merely makes evident what is fundamentally true for all people: That our sense of self is multiple, unstable, and constantly evolving.

In some instances, the complexity of diary subjectivity is expressed in a different form, through the use of a "we" perspective. For example, Michael Field was a pseudonym employed by the British writers Katharine Bradley (1846–1914) and Edith Cooper (1862–1913), who were aunt and niece, coauthors, and romantic partners. They published eight volumes of poetry under Field's name, but Bradley and Cooper took the case further. They referred to each other as "Michael" (Bradley) and "Field" (Cooper) and coauthored a diary in the persona of Michael Field. In doing so, they challenge the basic presupposition that diary writing is an individualistic activity and instead enact a pluralistic sense of self. Marion Thain argues the collaborative nature of the Field diary models queer authorial selfhood, wherein name, individuality, gender, and voice are proven to be unfixed markers, open to both playful reinvention and subversive critique (229).

For many, the multifaceted nature of the diary subject is one of the strongest appeals of the genre because it presents an opportunity for self-construction or re-creation. Recognizing that the written self can never be identical to the writing self, diarists embrace the diary as a tool for crafting a better version of themselves. This can be seen in the sub-category known as the spiritual diary, used by diarists to scrutinize their thoughts and behaviors according to religious values. However, the focus on a potential self is not limited to a religious context. Kimberly Harrison argues that secular diaries also exhibit the function of the genre to construct a new sense of identity. In her analysis of U.S. Confederate women's diaries, Harrison observes the implementation of "self-rhetoric" or the "personal, symbolic construction, revision, and maintenance of a rhetorical self" (15). According to Harrison, during times of personal or social upheaval, diarists turn to their diaries to proactively take on new roles or identities. Diaristic self-rhetoric may be designed to help diarists conform to dominant social ideals or it may be employed to subvert social norms by scripting counter-narratives. Ultimately, the concept of self-rhetoric prepares diary readers to examine how diarists persuade, encourage, discover, imagine, or even fictionalize themselves, rather than simply document themselves.

While the "I" focus of the diary can be productive, it also contributes to the popular perception that the genre is narcissistic. Gombrowicz's opening diary entries satirize the idea that all diary entries can be reduced to the word "me." As Elizabeth Hardwick put it, "There is no doubt that the diarist is the most egotistical of beings" (55). However, the perception of the self as complex, multifaceted, internally contradictory, and difficult to represent challenges this reductive assessment. The diarist's "I" covers a range of identities and may serve to create or imagine new ones. Moreover, the act of claiming selfhood through writing is laden with political and ideological significance. Criticizing the diary as a genre beset by self-absorption overlooks the power that self-representation grants to individuals who might be denied a sense of legitimacy and belonging in the wider world. To take yourself as the subject of your writing, even within an unpublished diary, is to claim yourself as significant and worthy of representation.

- How does the diary contribute to the author's construction of their subjectivity or identity?
- What version of the self does the diarist seek to record or create within their diary?
- Where does the multiplicity of the diary subject become evident? What do these moments reveal about the author, their diary, or the socio-historical context in which they are writing?

Diary Readers

The standard view is that diaries do not have readers. Although many believe that diaries are defined by their status as private texts, in Essential Question #2 I argue that the binary of public/private does not adequately account for the diverse ways in which diarists navigate the expectation of privacy. In this section, I focus on specific techniques diarists employ to engage with actual and imagined readers. I organize this discussion around several subcategories of diaries that address readers in ways that shape the form and content of the diary as a whole.

Self-addressed diaries are diaries in which the primary addressee is the author. Unlike other forms of autobiography, which take the self as the subject, some diaries present the self as subject and audience. Self-address can take the form of a literal address to the self, a rhetorical device that collapses the "I" of the writer and the "you" of the reader. For instance, Etty Hillesum (Dutch, 1914–1943) intersperses her diary with affectionate statements to herself: "You're not there by a long way yet, my girl"; "Well, Etty, you're just going to have to pick yourself up again" (August 4 and August 8, 1941). The theories of autobiographical subjectivity discussed in the previous section prompt us to consider how moments of self-address construct a version of the self. In

Hillesum's case, her reader-self is imagined as a sympathetic and encouraging friend but this figure can assume many forms: an idealized self, judgmental self, and so forth. The practice of self-address can also be designed to anticipate the possibility of re-reading by speaking to a future self who has returned to and is reflecting upon the past recorded in the diary. Some diarists address a future self and then respond in the future to their past self, turning the diary into a dialog across time.

Text-addressed diaries are diaries in which the diarist addresses the text as if it were an entity separate from the author. The well-known phrase "Dear Diary" demonstrates how this device can grant the text a status, an identity, and even a name distinct from the author's. Historians of the genre have not definitively established the origins of the "Dear Diary" address although they speculate that it is tied to the mass-production of diaries with the word "Diary" printed on their covers (Lejeune, *On Diary* 93). The practice of addressing the diary is designed to create an interlocutor for the diarist and, while this audience may be imaginary, it functions in many ways like a conventional textual audience: establishing a motive and justification for writing, a pretext for expository passages, and an invitation for response, even if unrealized. The phrase "Dear Diary" may also foreground the parallels between diary and epistolary genres, incorporating the letter's inherent sense of exchange into the nominal solitude of the diary. In addition, the modifier "dear" conveys the deep affection that many diarists have for their personal writing, regarding it as a friend or confidante. This device may insulate diarists from the accusation of narcissism so often lodged against the genre. By directing their affection toward the diary as an external entity, diarists might sidestep the explicit appearance of self-love.

For many diarists, the phrase "Dear Diary" is not sufficient. Instead, they construct a fictive persona for their diaries, complete with a separate name. The most famous example of a diarist naming her diary is Anne Frank's use of the affectionate term "Kitty" to refer to her diary. Frank explicitly addresses her intention to create an idealized interlocutor out of her diary: "I don't have a friend ... This is why I've started the diary ... I want the diary to be my friend, and I am going to call this friend *Kitty*"

(June 20, 1942). Frank's Kitty has inspired many other diarists to similarly name their diaries. For example, Zlata Filipović writes, "Hey Diary! You know what I think? Since Anne Frank called her diary Kitty, maybe I could give you a name too … I'm going to call you Mimmy" (March 30, 1992).

What does the device of addressing the diary accomplish for diarists? On the one hand, it can be understood to make visible how diarists address themselves. It externalizes the interior exchange that takes place when diarists narrate their lives or experiences. Lejeune has described the "Dear Diary" address as "a posture of self-address," suggesting that the text-addressed diary is actually another version of the self-addressed diary (*On Diary* 94). On the other hand, by naming and characterizing their diaries and/or fictive readers, diarists could be attempting to dictate how actual readers should engage with the text. Scholars debate the effect of this technique. For instance, Anne Frank's pretense of writing letters to Kitty has given rise to contrasting interpretations. Francine Prose argues that the pose "gave Anne a way of addressing her readers intimately and directly, in the second person: *you you you* … Reading Anne's diary, we become the friend" (91). By contrast, Nigel A. Caplan claims that Frank's use of Kitty restricts the reader's ability to connect to Frank. He writes, "Anne makes it clear that her reader can only ever be a spectator … [leaving] the reader of the Diary with the uncomfortable feeling of being a literary voyeur, reading misdirected letters" (93, 94). Is the reader of a text-addressed diary invited to feel as if they are the addressee, invited into an intimate relationship with the diarist? Or, is the reader excluded from the close relationship between the diarist and her addressee, to which the reader can only be an outside observer?

Diaries addressed to limited readers are diaries that are addressed to or shared with specific, known readers. These texts reject the premise that diaries must be private, although they attempt to restrict their readership to a select audience by limiting circulation to family members or friends. In the eighteenth and nineteenth centuries, sharing diaries in this way was part of a widespread manuscript culture that involved the composition, circulation, and performance of unpublished manuscripts in small social gatherings or among close companions. The exchange of diaries was particularly understood to enhance intimate relationships by producing what Rebecca Steinitz calls "diaristic intimacy" (91). For instance, Elizabeth Barrett Browning (English, 1806–1861) writes, "Last night I read some of my diary to Arabel [her sister] in bed! My diary is not meant to be read by any person except myself: but *she* deserves to be let behind the scenes" (January 2, 1832). W. N. P. Barbellion [a.k.a. Bruce Frederick Cummings] (English, 1889–1919) describes a more public exchange, as he invites friends to choose among the volumes of his diary for a post-dinner reading.

> I have … placed all my journals in a specially made cabinet. R--- came to dinner and after a glass or so of Beaune and a cigarette, I open my "coffin" (it is a long box with a brass handle at each end), and with some show of deliberation select a volume to read to him, drawing it from its division with lavish punctiliousness, and inquiring with an oily voice, "A little of 1912?" as if we were trying wines. R--- grins at the little farce and so encourages me.
>
> (September 25, 1914)

Anticipating an audience, even a small and select one, will impact a diarist's self-presentation in a variety of ways. It also shifts the function of the diary from a personal record to a social text meant to communicate with and be legible to an external audience.

Letter diaries are defined by their use of epistolary conventions and by the fact that they are typically sent through public mail services. Letter diaries (also known as *journal letters*) are usually addressed to a specific recipient but may also be shared with a wider audience, as it was customary in the past to read letters aloud or pass them to other readers. Like standard letters, letter diaries seek to overcome distances of space and time by bringing their readers into the "here" and "now" of the moment of composition. In addition, letter diaries entertain the possibility of a reply. Janet Altman argues that the defining feature of the letter is the expectation of reciprocity or response, what she terms the "epistolary pact" (89). Letter diaries navigate the reciprocal structure of letter writing in many ways. In some instances the communication exchange is unidirectional (from the diarist to their recipient) and in other instances it is multi-directional (back and forth between two or more writers). The letter diaries of Eugénie de Guérin (French, 1805–1848) were addressed to her brother, Maurice, and were designed to sustain the sibling bond despite physical distance. However, Maurice's importance to the writing process becomes especially evident after his death, when Eugénie continues to address her diary to her brother, describing it as an ongoing "tête-a-tête" despite the fact that the diaries would never reach their intended audience (February 11, 1840).

Collaborative diaries are another form of limited-address diary, coauthored by two or more people. These diaries contain more than one voice and, as such, challenge the standard view that diaries are the products of individual writers. Instead, collaborative diaries are further evidence of the function of the genre as a form of communication, designed to facilitate dialog and foster interpersonal relationships. Rachel Van Dyke (American, 1793–?) was encouraged to write a diary by her teacher, Ebenezer Grosvenor, whom she refers to as Mr. G. Under the guise of their student-teacher roles, the two embarked on a diary exchange that documents the progress of their flirtatious relationship. Mr. G responded to Van Dyke's diary entries in the margins, to which she added her responses – sometimes passing their diaries back and forth multiple times. They even developed a code to mask some of their more effusive interactions. The Van Dyke/Mr. G exchange foregrounds the function of collaborative diaries to establish emotional connections. Lucia McMahon characterizes their exchange as a form of "romantic readership" or an "intimate form of communicating and crafting a shared sense of identity" (310, 325). Shared diaries like Van Dyke's and those discussed above demonstrate that many diarists adapted the traditional introspective role of diary writing for an additional social purpose.

Diaries addressed to the public are diaries intended by their authors to be published and that speak directly to a general reader. The intention to publish is a pervasive theme within diary writing, although it contradicts the conventional idea of diaries as private. For some diarists, the expectation of a mass reading audience provides motivation for embarking upon and sticking with a diary writing practice. The publication of diaries in book form, which began in the eighteenth century, created an awareness of diary writing as a form of authorship and encouraged diarists to see themselves as participating in a literary tradition. Yet, publicity-seeking diarists remain aware of the perceived contradiction between their goals for publication and the traditional concept of the diary as written only for oneself. Attempting to address and reconcile this seeming contradiction is one of the defining features of public addressed diaries.

Marie Bashkirtseff was open about her pursuit of celebrity through her diary writing. In a preface she added ten years after beginning her diary, Bashkirtseff declared,

> What is the use of lying or pretending? … If I don't die young, I hope to become a great artist. If I do, I want my journal to be published. It cannot fail to be interesting. Does my anticipation of its being read spoil or destroy the merit of such a book? Not at all. … You can be sure, kind readers, that I show myself whole and entire.
>
> (May 1, 1884)

Throughout the diary, Bashkirtseff solicits her readers to witness her growing importance, depicting herself as an artistic genius deserving of an audience. Yet, her address to her readers is also playful and self-deprecating, puncturing her inflated self-rhetoric: "Dear and damned readers, don't let yourselves get tired of the story … I promise to do all I can to amuse you" (September 7, 1876). Such frank acknowledgments of literary ambitions won Bashkirtseff's diary passionate admirers but also exposed it to intense criticism by readers who were shocked by the absence of the humble self-effacement they expected in a young woman's diary. Instead, as Hilde Hoogenboom has shown, Bashkirtseff combined the conventions of the feminine diary with those of the publicity-seeking and implicitly male autobiography in order to represent a gender-bending sense of self (185). Bashkirtseff's imagined public is a necessary component of the version of herself she constructs through her diary writing.

The different forms of reader address enumerated above require us to interrogate the premise that all diarists desire privacy. Certainly, some diarists do not want to be read and take steps to resist readers such as codes, concealment strategies, self-censorship, and the editing or outright destruction of their diaries. But, for the most part, diarists are aware of the possibility of their diaries being read and this awareness influences their self-representation. As Judy Simons declares, "by their choice of mode as written documents all diaries imply readership" (10). At the same time, what diarists intend is not a reliable predictor of what actually happens. Diarists are not always able to control who gains access to their diaries. The public exposure of diary writing without the diarist's consent is a common historical phenomenon, evident in political scandals like those surrounding Roger Casement and Bob Packwood. While diaries sometimes contain evidence of their readership within the text or in their material form or chosen medium, scholars and students may have to look outside the text to determine whether and by whom a diary was read. This discussion of the convention of diary readers focuses on readership as an influence upon the composition of the text, as diarists negotiate with and adapt the figure of the reader for their own purposes.

- What impact does an anticipated readership have upon the text?
- How do critical concepts like audience, circulation, collaboration, publication, celebrity, or exposure help us to understand how the diarist thinks about or undertakes their diary writing?
- What evidence is there within the diary or within extratextual sources that the diary was intended to be or was read by others?

Diary Time

Chronological structure is perhaps the most conspicuous defining characteristic of diary writing. If you flip the pages of a text and observe it is segmented into parts with dated headings, you would have good reason to conclude you are holding a diary. Where does this convention come from and what does it teach us about the genre? Lejeune states that the practice of dating diary entries is a pivotal moment in the history of the genre; "the modern diary does not really become what it is until the day … the date moves out of the field of the enunciated [the diary entry] and into the field of the enunciation [the heading]" (*On Diary* 79). Stuart Sherman locates the origins of the chronologically dated diary in the eighteenth century, when time became regularized across the Western world due to new timekeeping technologies (the minute hand, the pocket watch), the standardization of networks like train schedules across wide geographic areas, and the rise of daily or dated publications like newspapers and magazines. According to Sherman, diaries were designed to help newly time-conscious individuals organize and control their temporal experience by documenting their lives on a diurnal or daily basis (34–35).

These historical roots explain the specific relationship that the diary has to past, present, and future. One notable time effect of the diurnal diary results from the diarist's lack of foreknowledge about the future. Because diarists are unable to predict what will happen next, it is impossible for them to use the literary technique of foreshadowing. Arthur Inman (American, 1895–1963) explains this problem to his imagined diary readers:

> Look a line in advance of the one I am writing on, and all is blank. Tomorrow, I may record the fulfillment of all desires, or some other hand may inscribe for me "Finis." You who read every entry, read with the realization in mind that when it was written, I never knew what cryptic events would form unguessable sequence.
>
> (August 25, 1922)

At the same time that diarists cannot represent the future, neither do they generally seek to represent the past. Although some diarists may use the space of their diaries to record past events or to reflect on the meaning or significance of the past, diaries are characterized as *nonretrospective*, or not primarily designed to present a narrative of the past. Many other autobiographical genres are intended to provide a retrospective overview of the writer's life. In a memoir, for example, the writer looks backward over and makes sense of the past from the standpoint of "now." By contrast, diaries are preoccupied with the present moment. They seek to represent the "now" as it occurs – or as it just occurred, immediately before the diarist takes up their pen. Critics have characterized this temporal orientation as the "eternal present" or "true present" of diary time (Lejeune, *On Diary* 54; Abbott, *Diary* 30). Sarah Manguso (American, 1974–) describes this present tense orientation as a feeling of "ongoingness," as if the present moment always and endlessly needs to be recorded (4). Yet, while chronology gives diary writing motive, structure, and stylistic evenness, it is also inherently fragmenting as the dated headings that organize the diary also divide it into parts, a fact often made visually evident by the blank lines or white space between entries. The temporal self represented by the diary thus possesses the same attributes of multiplicity and complexity we have seen in the diary subject.

Although it is common to associate the diary entry with the temporal unit of the day and to expect entries to be presented in a chronological fashion, this is by no means the only way diaries can be organized. Alternative organizations of time can be seen, for instance, in the practice of writing monthly or yearly summaries either in addition to or in place of daily entries. Ernesto "Che" Guevara (Argentine, 1928–1967) used monthly reflections he called "Analysis of the Month" in his Bolivian war diaries to articulate the positive achievements of his guerrilla campaign, often in contrast to the more somber contents of his daily entries. When Nuha al-Radi (Iraqi, 1941–2004) began keeping her diary to document the United States' bombing of Iraq, she initially counted the days as Day 1, Day 2, etc. instead of employing dated headings in order to clearly distinguish the time of war from the regular flow of time. Heidi Julavits (American, 1968–) rejects chronology altogether in *The Folded Clock*, a reprinting of diary entries that places them in a nonchronological sequence, disrupting the prospect of a coherent memoir. As these examples demonstrate, the expectation that diaries will be diurnal and chronological is a convention that many diarists explore, challenge, and experiment with.

- How does the diarist convey the temporality of their diary?
- In what ways does the diarist employ, revise, or reject the conventional structure of diary time?
- What does the diarist's representation of time reveal about their sense of self, or their place within larger temporal structures (history, genealogy, tradition, etc.)?

Beginnings, Endings, Middles

Diaries often begin with a declaration of purpose. For diary readers these declarations are valuable keys for unlocking the writer's intent, their choice of content or format, and their view of themselves as writers. James Boswell (British, 1740–1795) begins,

> [Keeping a daily journal] will give me a habit of application and improve me in expression and knowing that I am to record my transactions will make me more careful to do well. Or if I should go wrong, it will assist me in resolutions of doing better.
>
> (November 15, 1762)

Charlotte Forten Grimké (American, 1837–1914) begins,

> A wish to record the passing events of my life, which, even if quite unimportant to others, naturally possess great interest to myself, and of which it will be pleasant to have some remembrance, has induced me to commence this journal.
>
> (May 1854)

Openings such as these provide a lens through which to interpret the text that follows.

While the beginning of a diary is an occasion for the diarist to spell out their goals, other beginnings also provide opportunities for self-reflection, including the beginning of a new year, birthdays, the start of a new volume of a diary, or other meaningful dates throughout the calendar year, such as anniversaries. Often, such moments of restarting, renewing, or commemoration provoke a mode of diary writing that rises above the daily record and, as such, can serve as a roadmap for readers who seek to understand the diarist and their writing strategies. In a sense, each diary entry is also a new beginning. The choice to implement the diary's formulaic patterns is one made each time the diarist writes and therefore can be understood to present a recurring opportunity for the diarist to recommit to the goals of their diary.

Diary endings, on the other hand, present a problem. Lejeune states "the diary is experienced as writing without an end" (*On Diary* 188). Some diaries come with a preordained endpoint: Travel diaries typically end with the return home, preformatted calendar diaries conclude at the end of the year, and so forth. But most diaries are written with the expectation that there will be another diary entry tomorrow. Diaries do not, as a rule, entertain the option of ending, as the genre's relationship to chronological time compels the text ever forward. As with beginnings, however, there are many small endings throughout a diary: the end of a calendar year, the end of a specific period of one's life, the end of a diary volume, and the end of each diary entry. Lejeune describes these as moments of "partial closure," which form a kind of relay that requires the writer to start and end over and over again (189). Breaks or interruptions in the relay or in the diarist's established pattern of writing often provoke apologies and explanations, passages that document the writer's awareness that diaries are not meant to end.

While the genre provides few formulas for closure, diaries do end, and how endings are marked or unmarked are worthy of analysis. W. N. P. Barbellion documents the decline of his heath, writing in his final diary entry, "Self-disgust" (October 21, 1917).

The lines that follow read: "Finis. / [Barbellion died on December 31.]" However, this dramatic conclusion was a fictional device. Barbellion lived for two more years, long enough to publish his diary and to write a sequel. Barbellion's earliest readers, taking the declaration of his death as truth, were outraged to learn that he was still alive. But the genre's conventions might have taught them that marked conclusions are often literary contrivances or opportunities for crafting a specific version of the diarist's life or identity. Unmarked conclusions can also be powerful acts of communication. The final entry in Virginia Woolf's diary reads "L [her husband Leonard] is in the middle of trimming the rhododendrons" (March 24, 1941). She committed suicide three days later. Elizabeth Podnieks describes reading Woolf's final diary entries in the original manuscript and discovering that

> her last entry is … near the beginning of a new diary volume, in which she had ruled her own margins on each page … Woolf had set up the diary as a book which she had intended to fill.
>
> (105–6)

The blank diary pages that follow Woolf's last entry serve as a poignant testament to the problem that the end of life presents to the unending project of diary writing.

While diary beginnings and endings are rich with interpretative possibility, the primary register of diary writing is the middle. Diaries are defined by their middleness: They reside in the middle of time, the middle of life, and so forth (Sinor 56). A diary's middleness is often conveyed through the author's use of *parataxis*, a mode of writing that treats all subject matter as equal. Elizabeth Drinker (American, 1735–1807) captures the list-like style of parataxis, which flattens distinction even in places where readers might expect it. One of her diary entries reads, "my child very restless last Night slept none myself, till after day – a report prevails at present, that independence is granted: believed by many. – John Hopkins junr. din'd with us …" (May 4, 1782). Drinker describes her sick child, the end of the Revolutionary War, and a dinner guest without emphasizing one over the other, rhetorically placing herself in the middle of experience. The use of parataxis erases difference within diary entries but it also establishes a style of representation that cuts across entries as the repetitiveness of sequential diary entries can also erase distinctions between individual days. The diary's ability to represent middleness distinguishes it from autobiography, which typically imposes an arc of development, change, and resolution upon the narrated life. Felicity Nussbaum writes, while autobiography requires a "transformation from a former self to a new fixed self," the diary "creates and tolerates crisis in perpetuity" (134). For diary readers, it is necessary to learn to read middles instead of only focusing on beginnings or endings. The diary's openness to unresolved experience invites us to explore the diary as a genre without predictable boundaries.

- How does the diary begin? What does the beginning indicate about the diarist's goals, intentions, self-presentation, or circumstances?
- How does the diary end? What does the ending indicate about the diarist's relationship to diary writing, or to the self-rhetoric they have implemented in the diary?
- How does the diary communicate its middleness? What is the diarist in the middle of? What do these devices reveal about how identity or experience are represented in the text?

Space and Image

Diarists do not only make meaning through language or writing, they also make meaning through their creative use of the space of the page. Equally, they make meaning through visual images: drawings, diagrams, maps, photographs, newspaper clippings, and so forth. These elements of the diary may work in concert with the written text, or may alter our understanding of the written text. Paying attention to the spaces and images within a diary is another means of unlocking its meaning.

Exploring the space of a diary has to do with the material arrangement or spatial composition of the text on the page. This is particularly relevant when reading manuscript diaries, but may also be useful with print or digital texts, depending on their formats. Many diaries seek to dictate to writers how their words should appear on the page, for instance, preprinted calendar diaries that allocate a certain amount of space for each diary entry. Diarists employing preprinted diaries have to decide whether to honor these established parameters, or to adapt or violate them. For many diarists, filling in a preset space creates a comforting sense of regularity and accomplishment. For others, the material dimensions of the diary present challenges that have to be overcome in order for diarists to express themselves. Marginal spaces are especially important: Does the diarist preserve the white spaces of the margin? Or, does the diarist write in the vertical margin, and for what purpose? Does the diarist create a horizontal margin between entries? Attending to the marginal spaces of individual diary pages also encourages attention to the marginal spaces of diary notebooks. The opening and closing pages of print books are known as "paratexts," which Gérard Genette describes as functioning as a threshold or doorway that ushers the reader into and out of the text (1–2). Historically, the paratexts of preprinted diaries have included title pages, prefaces, calendars, almanacs, astronomical cycles, and lists of major holidays at the beginning of the notebook and pages for recording budgets, expenses, addresses, important dates, and memoranda at the end. The notes made by diarists in these marginal pages may appear fundamentally disconnected from the central diary, but it is worth considering how these parts of the text relate and why diarists place certain information in the text's margins. Of course, many diarists use blank notebooks, make their own diaries, or employ word processing software or digital apps to write their diaries. These spatial concerns can be extended to their writing as well: How does the diarist create and delimit the space of each entry? How does the diarist mark the beginnings and endings of their diary as a material or virtual object?

Diarists also use visual images to make meaning within their diaries. Many writers insert materials in their material diaries, using them like scrapbooks, commonplace books, or photograph albums. Some turn their diaries into archival repositories, inserting letters or newspaper clippings that illustrate their lives. Others paste in images from advertisements or favorite quotes, or items such as pressed flowers or memorabilia. Ellen Gruber Garvey characterizes this kind of textual production as "writing with scissors," the practice of "finding, sifting, analyzing, and recirculating" material written or produced by others to compose a new text (4). According to Garvey, these materials take on new meaning when they are inserted into new contexts (such as a diary) and placed next to different kinds of writing (diary entries or other interleaved materials). Essentially, the compiler "writes" through the combination of texts, objects, and language, a practice that transforms authorship into a polyvocal and multimodal phenomenon. Through this practice, diarists make use of other's voices or modes of expression to represent themselves.

Many diarists also illustrate their diaries. Rather than collecting and reusing images created by others, they draw, sketch, and paint within the pages of their diaries. Most illustrated diaries display a combination of image and written text. The World War II diaries of Molly Lamb Bobak (Canadian, 1920–2014) take the form of illustrated newspaper pages, with headlines, separate columns, and captioned images. (Figure 3.1) For Bobak, the mock-newspaper format provided a justification for the arrangement of image and text, while other diarists intersperse their diary entries with illustrations in a less formal way. In either case, it is the interplay between image and text that constitutes the meaning of the diary, inviting readers to read between and across the two modes of representations. Other diarists dispense with the conventional written text of the diary and rely primarily on image to narrate their lives. As Julia Watson explains, visual diaries are capable of communicating "feelings and perceptions that may be not only unvoiced but inarticulable in ordinary language" (24). For example, Takuichi Fujii (American,

No1 EDITION
PUBLISHED IN BETWEEN SERVING SOLDIERS IN THE CANTEEN - 6 - 10 AT NIGHT

W110278.

PUBLISHED DAILY.
VANCOUVER BARRACKS
NOVEMBER 22ND 1942.

GIRL TAKES DRASTIC STEP!

"YOUR IN THE ARMY NOW" AS MEDICAL TEST OKAYED.

FLASH …… WEDNESDAY, NOVEMBER 18, 1942 – VANCOUVER BARRACKS …… On Wednesday, the 18 of November, Civilian Lamb offered herself unwillingly and willingly, willy nilly, to the C.W.A.C. When reporters interviewed her on Wednesday night they found her in a mental state. "I've never known so much misery" she stated torturedly. "Except when I didn't win the Scolarship at school. After they said my second medical was good I was sent to different floors of the Barracks to get an arm band, a knife and fork and spoon, a mattress, 3 blankets, a pillow and two sheets. I went through long dark corridors with an experienced Private who told me I must learn to walk faster and didn't answer any of my bewildered questions.

THE BEDROOM

"What about accomodation?" asked reporters. "Well," laughed the now happy Pte. Lamb, "I found a bare concrete room with twelve iron cots (double deckers) in it. There was a fine view of the city because it was on the twelfth floor. But I didn't notice. I just put my things on the top of the first iron bed and followed the Private to a Sergeant-major who took me to my work.

THE WORK.

"And what was the work?" queried the press. "If you're not bored" continued Private Lamb "I'll tell you about it – I was taken to a noisy canteen, (CON'T ON PAGE II COLUMN I.)

PRIVATE LAMB LOOKING AT RAIN 5:30 (17:30 ARMY TIME) OUTSIDE BARRACKS.

Figure 3.1 Molly Lamb Bobak Diary. Molly Lamb enters the Army, November 22, 1942 © Library and Archives Canada. Reproduced with the permission of Library and Archives Canada. Source: Library and Archives Canada. Credit: Molly Lamb Bobak/Molly Lamb Bobak and Bruno Bobak fonds / e006078933

1891–1964) composed an illustrated diary about the experiences he and his family faced when they were placed in an interment camp during World War II. Although many of his ink drawings include captions, image is Fugii's central mode of expression. Yet, the chronological sequence of events (the diary begins with the forced evacuation of Japanese Americans and ends with their train ride home) and the personal point of view of each illustration confirm that Fugii's text was a diary. (Figure 3.2) Fugii's diary is evidence of the ways the diary genre both borrows from and accommodates a wide range of visual representational methods. These modes of representation link the traditional diary to other kinds of "autographics" (Whitlock and Poletti v), including graphic narratives like comic books and graphic memoirs (discussed in Chapter 4) and digital diaries like blogs and social media (discussed in Chapter 5).

- How does the diarist arrange their written text on the space of the page? How and why do they establish, utilize, or destabilize textual boundaries like preset areas for diary entries, margins, or blank space?
- What kinds of visual materials does the diarist include, and why? How do interleaved materials or illustrations shape the meaning of the text?

Silences and Concealments

Sometimes diarists communicate more through absences, omissions, or erasures than through exposition. This section focuses on two such modes of communication – *silences* (what is left out) and *concealments* (what is included, but hidden). Obviously, diarists leave a great deal out and it is important to not over-read the diarist's inability to document all aspects of their life. It is particularly important to be attentive of diaries that may appear to be silent on important topics but are actually employing an abbreviated style of diary writing. Elizabeth Hampsten describes these as "nothing happened" diaries: diaries that focus on the everyday, the mundane, or the repetitive (4). Readers searching

Figure 3.2 Takuichi Fujii Diary, 1942–1945. Original caption: "Indeed, this is an odd door. The lock is on the outside. I see that this relocation center is a prison." Courtesy of Sandy and Terry Kita

for what is left out of "nothing happened" diaries may conclude that the diarist is hiding "something." However, it is important to distinguish between an ordinary mode of diary writing and the specific use of silence to convey meaning.

Silences take two forms: *marked silences* and *unmarked silences*. Marked silences are those that are conspicuous in the text: absences of information, gaps in the diarist's pattern of writing, or unexplained changes in the diarist's life or self-representation. Very often, diarists acknowledge silences directly. After a gap of one year in his diary, Stepan Filippovich Podlubny (Russian, 1914–) writes,

> No one will ever know how I made it through the year 1937. No one will know because not a single day of my life this year has been illuminated in this so-called diary … I'll cross it out and banish it from my mind though the black spot[,] the massive ugly black spot like a thick blood stain on my clothes, will be with me most likely for the rest of my life.
>
> (December 6, 1937)

The editors of his diary state that this marked silence references Podlubny's role as an informer for the Russian secret police (291). Yet, even without this extratextual context, readers could interpret his silence as a meaningful way of documenting, without explicitly describing, a powerful secret.

Unmarked silences are far more challenging to identify because they may only be visible to the diarist. A. M. Duncan-Wallace (Scottish, n.d.) kept a diary during his interment in Singapore during World War II. The typed transcript of the diary includes a preface in which Duncan-Wallace identifies a series of "intentional omissions." He writes, "My reason for omitting all these very significant facts is evident. I feared that my diary might one day fall into the hands of the Japanese" ("Introduction"). While the gaps in Duncan-Wallace's chronological record would be visible to readers, the silences he retrospectively lists may not be readily apparent. Reading unmarked silences relies upon information provided by the author or other extratextual sources that can help to contextualize the diary. Yet, readers should proceed with caution, aware of the pitfalls of searching for what is not there or cannot be known.

Concealment strategies are employed by diarists to simultaneously include and hide. Codes are one of the primary modes of concealment within diaries, but because I discuss codes in detail in Essential Question #3, here I focus on alternative strategies. Some concealments are employed during the writing process. For example, a diarist may develop methods for obscuring the meaning or references of certain words or phrases through blank spaces or abbreviated words (example: S----). Or, this might appear as veiled or unspecific language, which would only be comprehensible to the diarist. Alternatively, concealment strategies can be implemented after the fact such as when a diarist or other individual retroactively alters a diary to omit or cover up what was once recorded openly. Retroactive concealments might take the form of crossed out passages, erased words or phrases, torn or cut out pages, or other manipulations of a diary manuscript. It can be challenging to determine who made such changes to the text: Was it the diarist, a known or unknown reader, a family member, an editor? While any of these possibilities would be worth analyzing, they represent different forms of authorship, collaboration, or editorial intervention and should be interpreted fittingly. In the absence of clear information about who implemented the concealment strategy, readers must again exercise caution in drawing conclusions about its meaning.

One of the great ironies of concealment strategies is that they tend to draw attention to the very things that writers mean to cover up. Readers are fascinated by the mystery inherent in missing pages, crossed out words, and blank spaces, and in some cases diaries are read primarily through the lens of their omissions. For example, interpretations of the *Grasmere Journal* by Dorothy Wordsworth (British, 1771–1855) hinge significantly on one diary entry, which recounts Dorothy's reaction to her brother William's marriage and which has been used as evidence in the ongoing debate about whether their relationship was incestuous. The fact that the entry was scratched out is seen as a key component in this debate, the concealment strategy itself viewed by many as a form of confession. Examples like this indicate how the attempt to conceal is often interpreted as a form of revelation. Following a psychoanalytic framework, the act of concealment is thought to speak more loudly of the individual's true motives or intents than an open declaration. So why do diarists or their readers/editors use blatant concealment strategies? As we see with coded diaries, these methods are double-edged modes of representation, simultaneous acts of record and reticence. Both silences and concealment strategies return us to the question of diary readership discussed above because they would appear to be forms of expression only necessary if the diarist anticipates a possible reader. Diarists who silence, censor, or edit themselves implicitly acknowledge an audience, while nevertheless stopping short of the most effective way of limiting their readership: complete destruction of their diaries. The power of the diary as a form of self-narrative is evident in the contradictory drives to record yet conceal.

- Identify marked silences in the diary: How are they indicated, and why? How does the diarist employ silence to communicate or record?
- Identify concealment strategies in the diary: Is it possible to identify the agent? What do these textual features reveal about the diarist, their intended or anticipated audience, or the history of the text?

Common Ways of Misreading Diaries

Diary readers are faced with many challenges including extremely long diaries that sprawl across decades; "nothing happened" diaries that seem repetitive and uninteresting; deeply interior diaries that resist readers' comprehension, and so on. Faced with these challenges, scholars and critics of the diary have at times employed interpretative methods that reinforce literary hierarchies, promote narrow perceptions of what diaries are, and fail to respect the genre's history or defining conventions.

Storying is a way of misreading diaries that is based on the assumption that diaries will and should tell stories, and that readers have the responsibility to find and extract the story lurking within a diary. Sinor describes the desire "to story" (as a verb) a diary as arising from the belief that "[b]ecause neither the text nor the writer can speak, someone must speak for them, story for them" (16). Storying a diary involves imposing a plot upon the life narrative, especially one that follows conventional autobiographical arcs of development, change, or self-discovery (88). It also involves highlighting moments of drama, intrigue, struggle, or surprise over the regular routines of daily life – a move that is particularly tempting when reading diaries that employ parataxis to flatten the distinctions between ordinary and extraordinary life experiences. Oriented toward story, readers are trained to extract extraordinary moments from ordinary ones, and to place them in a sequential and plot-like order – even if doing so runs against the diarist's own chosen patterns or modes of self-representation. Of course, some diarists story their own diaries, particularly those that rewrite or revise their diaries for readers or publication, in which case the diarist's storying strategies themselves become topics for critical analysis. Otherwise, readers run the risk of making the diary something it is not, rather than respecting and engaging with the diary for what it is.

Snippetotomy is another form of misreading diaries, and refers to the practice of "snipping" out from a large text only those details or passages that are relevant to the reader's interest. Harry Berger defines snippetotomy as "readings of small excerpts … [which] are made to stand for the wholes of which they are parts" (563). Snipping a diary involves dipping into the text, extracting selected themes, topics, or information, and building an interpretation of the text based on these decontextualized parts. It is a form of reading that is particularly evident in the practice of treating diaries as historical repositories of facts or data, while failing to consider the text as a whole. Berger and others identify this as a common phenomenon in readings of Samuel Pepys's diary. Sherman argues that Pepys's diary is "raid[ed] as a database" by historians searching for details about life in the seventeenth century (31). The unique status of Pepys's diary (claimed by many as the first and most exemplary historical diary) contributes to this treatment of the text, but it is a practice that can be seen in many diary analyses. While scholars and students may have to be selective when writing about a lengthy diary, they should limit the scope of their claims in light of this fact.

Psychologizing is the final and most complicated form of misreading diaries. It is one of the great temptations of diary analysis to assume as readers we are equipped to diagnose the diarist's psychological state of mind and unmask their secrets or subconscious desires. The field of psychoanalytic literary criticism is a robust and influential one, and readers trained within this field are equipped to explore how writers reveal deep meanings and motives in their choice of language or symbols. Readers who lack this training are cautioned against jumping to conclusions regarding what diarists "really" mean, particularly if the interpretation hinges on a snippet of text that appears unusually self-revealing. Although diaries are thought to be uniquely designed to give readers access to the true self of the diarist, the discussion of conventions in this chapter demonstrates that both the "truth" and the "self" of diary writing are constructs that serve multiple and at times contradictory purposes. A focus on the constructed text acknowledges that the biographical author remains permanently inaccessible. Even the most public-facing or audience-seeking diaries will have boundaries past which readers cannot go. The desire to know everything is a powerful incentive that drives much diary reading but readers are best served by developing a degree of comfort with the unknowable dimensions of the diary.

Essential Question #3: Why Are Some Diaries Written in Code?

Many diarists employ codes in their diaries, even though this technique challenges influential preconceptions about the genre. If the diary is private and has no readers, why would a diarist need to resort to a code? If the diary is a repository for truthful self-revelation, why should any content be coded? And if diarists want to hide something, why wouldn't they simply not write it down in the first place? In order to answer these questions, we should begin by distinguishing between different kinds of codes (verbal, visual, symbolic, numerical) and the different functions that they serve (convenience, concealment).

Some diary codes are designed for the writer's convenience, rather than to hide content. Diarists develop codes, shorthand, and abbreviations in order to facilitate their diary writing, particularly for the purpose of quickly referencing commonly repeated topics, words, or names. For instance, Elizabeth Drinker refers to many people in her diary by their initials, including her husband, Henry Drinker, who is "HD" throughout most of the diary. Drinker's use of initials is a mechanism for communicating familiarity or intimacy: Names indicated by initials refer to those with whom she interacts frequently, while names spelled out in full are acquaintances or strangers. Some codes for convenience appear in visual or symbolic form. Robert Hooke (British, 1635–1703) drew alchemical and astronomical symbols in his diary to document weather patterns. Many women diarists used visual codes to track their menstrual cycles, such as the flowers Annie Ray drew in the margins of her diaries (119). Codes for convenience tell a story about the patterns of diarists' lives, allowing readers to map networks of relations, movements across time and space, and recurring experiences or obsessive preoccupations. However, even functional codes present challenges to readers, who may not be able to deduce their referents. While it is important to distinguish them from codes designed to conceal, codes of convenience can end up being equally illegible to readers.

Codes of concealment serve a different function. They are "disguising strategies," meant to simultaneously document and veil (Vermeer). While these may appear to be contradictory impulses, the use of codes provides diarists with a means of uniting them. Often codes are necessitated by the political circumstances in which the diarist writes. Ada Gobetti (Italian, 1902–1968) kept a diary of her activities in the Italian Resistance during World War II, writing "skeletal notes in a cryptic English that was almost unintelligible" in order to prevent enemy forces from interpreting it (27). Gobetti's technique of writing in a foreign language is one of the most common forms of diary coding. Writing in a foreign language can be easy for a bilingual diarist but also very effective as a code, assuming that readers are unfamiliar with the language. Zhang Xianliang (Chinese, 1936–2014) composed his diary while he was imprisoned in a labor camp, conscious that the diary was subject to surveillance. He wrote a highly selective account of his experiences but occasionally included coded information, legible only to himself. He ends one diary entry with an exclamation mark and clarifies in the accompanying explanatory text, "You may note that there was a kind of code in the diary: I cut hemp from 30 July to 5 August, but only on the 30th of July did I write an exclamation mark after the entry. This punctuation was imbued with gratitude" (109). Zhang's exclamation mark indicates the challenges that codes present to readers. Without his explanation, it would be almost impossible to reconstruct the meaning of that single act of punctuation, as the code effectively prevents both surveillance and interpretation.

It will come as no surprise that the vast majority of diary codes are employed to represent sex and sexuality, indicating the special status these topics have within diaristic discourse. Samuel Pepys wrote his entire diary in shorthand but employed a mixture of several foreign languages for passages in which he records his sexual activities. William

Matthews explains, "This language is basically Spanish (of a dictionary kind, and therefore considerably ungrammatical); but into it are mixed words from several other languages: English, French, and occasionally Dutch, Italian, Latin, and Greek," and into which Pepys would insert extra nonsensical letters ("The Diary" lxi). Anne Lister (British, 1791–1840) documented her gender-bending identity and sexual relationships with women in her diaries, employing what she called a "secret alphabet" or a "crypt hand," a code that combined Greek letters with visual symbols of her own design (May 22, 1817; August 31, 1820). Lister's bold transgression of gender norms brought her notoriety during her lifetime, and she was acutely aware that her sexuality opened her up to social condemnation or worse. At the same time, Lister shared the key to her code with lovers to use in their epistolary correspondence, indicating that it also constituted a separate language that signified inclusion within a same-sex community. John Maynard Keynes (British, 1883–1946) kept two simultaneous diaries recording his sexual relations but only one is legible. The second diary involves tabulating his activities under three categories labeled C, A, and W, but as of yet the meaning of these letters and the numbers listed under each category is unknown. Evan Zimroth speculates that the records constitute a rating system, through which Keynes scored his sexual encounters (20), but the code remains effectively encrypted.

Ironically, while diary codes may be designed to hide certain sexual content, they frequently have the contrary effect of drawing more attention to it. Many readers of Pepys's diary have noted that the coded passages stand out from the rest of the text. Aaron Kunin writes, it is "as though someone had gone through the manuscript and underlined all the good parts" (206). Readers are often fascinated by codes, intrigued by the challenge of breaking them, and convinced that anything rendered in code must be of more significance than the surrounding plaintext. Given the possibility of increased scrutiny, why do diarists write in code and particularly about sex? The temptation may be to interpret coded passages about sex as communicating a sense of shame or guilt, but while this may be the case for some, it does not explain all motives. Attitudes toward sex, sexual identity, and specific sex acts change over time. For instance, the stigma attached to non-heterosexual identities or relationships during certain historical periods could be a strong incentive for gay, lesbian, and bisexual diarists to employ a code. Yet Matt Cook argues that for gay diarists, the choice to include detailed or coded descriptions of their sex lives, or to exclude them altogether, are all equally ways of "securing a sense of homosexual selfhood" (202). At the same time, there are many diaries in which authors (gay and straight) write openly, explicitly, and even boastfully about their sexual experiences, so masking this content is only one expressive option.

There are many reasons diarists use codes:

To carve out a deeper level of privacy within the space of personal writing.
To conform to societal norms regarding appropriate and inappropriate written subject matter.
To display their gentility, respectability, or discretion.
To enact and perform a sense of intimacy with readers to whom the code is legible.
To signal the contested status of the text or the life it represents within specific historical or political contexts.
To provoke readers' curiosity and draw their attention.
To indicate the importance of certain information to the diarist.
To playfully or proudly demonstrate their linguistic or encryption skills
– and so on.

Just as codes take many forms, the different motives and intentions for employing codes indicate the complex functions that these writing strategies perform within the diary.

4 Reading Diary Fiction

For as long as there have been diaries, there have been writers adapting the diary to tell fictional stories. Diaries appear in a wide variety of fictional genres – poetry, plays, musicals, operas, films, TV, podcasts – but they appear most abundantly in the novel and the short story, narrative forms that are particularly suited to borrow the defining characteristics of the diary: the first person point of view, chronological structure, and intimate subject matter. Despite the fact that these characteristics transfer easily to many forms of fiction, adapting the diary for fictional purposes presents a number of creative challenges. Authors have to decide to what extent they want to follow the structure, style, and conventions of the diary, or to what extent these characteristics present obstacles for their storytelling. Lorna Martens writes that diary fiction "manifests a continual tension" between imitating nonfiction diaries and inventing new or hybrid modes of representation (51–52). The choices that authors make when adapting the diary open up lines of literary analysis, particularly for readers who are knowledgeable about the conventions of the nonfiction diary.

What makes a literary text a work of diary fiction? Most commonly, the story is entirely in the form of a diary, replicating the chronological sequence of dated diary entries. Diary fiction also includes stories that are only partially in diary form. H. Porter Abbott argues that 50 percent of a text has to be in diary form for it to be considered diary fiction (*Diary* 208), but this is not a standard accepted by other scholars, who place more emphasis on the significance of the diary to the overall story (Martens, Prince). According to this wider view, diary fiction may also include stories in which a diary serves as an important plot point, even though the story never takes diary form and, as a result, the diary's contents are concealed from the reader. This can include stories in which characters read, discuss, contemplate, search for, find, hide, or destroy diaries. The flexibility of the diary fiction label reflects the location of these works within the equally broad and flexible category of *autobiographical fiction*, works of fiction that either closely parallel the biography of the author or that borrow techniques from autobiography, usually with the intention of encouraging readers to view the story as being about the author's real life. Sometimes referred to as *autofiction*, this category also includes fictional memoir and biography, and epistolary fiction. While works of autobiographical fiction can be interpreted using the same techniques applied to general fiction, most scholars agree that readers must pay particular attention to the ways in which authors navigate between autobiography and fiction, utilizing both despite the fact that they may seem antithetical.

This chapter prepares readers to interpret diary fiction by identifying the principal ways in which authors adapt the nonfiction diary in novels and short stories. Most literary criticism on this topic focuses on the *diary novel*, or novels in diary form, but I prefer the term *diary fiction* because it includes short stories, comics, and graphic novels, among other kinds of storytelling. While my discussion will primarily address novels and short stories, readers are encouraged to apply the terms and concepts outlined in this chapter widely, testing their relevance to audio, digital, performative, and visual texts that are inspired by diaries. I begin by providing a brief historical overview of diary fiction before outlining four major conventions of diary fiction. I proceed to discuss four thematic areas for the study of diary fiction: gender, sex, and sexuality; colonialism and postcolonialism; young adult fiction; and graphic narrative. I conclude by addressing the question, what can diary fiction teach us about nonfiction diaries?

A Very Short History of Diary Fiction

The history of diary fiction follows closely the history of the diary, particularly as it developed in the West. Scholars generally identify diary fiction as beginning to emerge as a recognizable literary form during the eighteenth century, at the same time that nonfiction diary writing gained popularity and nonfiction diaries began to be published. In other words, as the diary became more familiar to the general reading public, authors began to explore how it could be adapted for fictional purposes. A major transformative moment occurs towards the middle of the eighteenth century, when the novel originates as a literary form. The earliest novels frequently mimicked preexisting forms of writing. This is a common strategy whenever a new kind of media emerges: Creators present new media in the form of older media in order to help audiences accept the new. In the case of the novel, novelists sought to facilitate readers' interest in this new kind of writing by incorporating older modes of expression, including letters and diaries. In fact, scholars like J. Paul Hunter argue that the diary was a necessary predecessor for the novel (303). Many of the earliest novels are *epistolary novels* (in the form of letters) or *diary novels* (in the form of a diary), or a mix of the two genres. Epistolary and diary novels share so many characteristics that some scholars view them as interchangeable, particularly in the case of epistolary novels in which the recipient never responds, known as *single-author epistolary novels*. In these novels, although the protagonist purports to write letters to another person, the lack of response results in their letters taking on the diaristic function of self-address. The nonfiction letter diary, discussed in Chapter 3, substantiates the idea that letters and diaries are linked genres and provides additional guidance regarding how to interpret hybrid epistolary-diary novels.

Diary novels play a significant role in the development and increasing prominence of the novel within Western literary history, embodying many of the themes and styles of writing that would come to define the genre. One of the first and most influential English novels, Daniel Defoe's *Robinson Crusoe* (1719), is told partially through Crusoe's diary, written after he was stranded on an island by a shipwreck. *Robinson Crusoe* and other adventure tales were rivaled in popularity by novels of seduction in diary form such as Samuel Richardson's *Pamela* (1740), an epistolary novel that converts to a diary when the main character is held captive by the man who is trying to seduce her. Although she keeps writing letters, the fact that they are not sent to her intended audience transforms them into diary entries. The seduction narrative was a transatlantic phenomenon, taken up by American authors like Susanna Rowson, who inserts a diary in her epistolary novel *Sincerity* (1803–1804) in order to document the heroine's mental disintegration as a result of being wrongly labeled an unfaithful wife. The diary form was also central to early novels that focused on the interior lives of tragic individuals, exemplified by Johann Wolfgang von Goethe's *The Sorrows of Young Werther* (1774). Although *Werther* is an epistolary novel, the confessional style of the protagonist's writing strongly evokes the diary and many of the novels written in imitation of *Werther* are explicitly in diary form.

Although some scholars argue that diary novels declined both in number and significance after the eighteenth century (Martens), others contend that the diary continued to play an important role in nineteenth-century literature, especially within Romantic and Gothic fiction (Delafield, Steinitz). Anne Brontë's *The Tenant of Wildfell Hall* (1848) is a diary-within-a-diary novel in which the diarist-narrator reads the diary of his love interest, a device that builds upon the belief that sharing diaries cements intimate bonds between individuals. Novels like Wilkie Collins's *The Moonstone* (1868) and Bram Stoker's *Dracula* (1897) interweave multiple diaries written by different characters who offer different points of view on the central mystery. This structure places readers in the role of detective or investigator, sorting through the various accounts in order to uncover the truth. The use of the diary to document the trials of the romantic individual can be seen in André Gide's *The Notebooks of André Walter* (1891), which is composed of two diaries: A white notebook that describes the start of a love affair and a black notebook that describes the aftermath of the affair. It is also during the nineteenth century that authors began to utilize the diary for the purpose of exploring the complexity of the human mind, particularly through self-narratives by deranged, antisocial, and amoral individuals. Nikolay Gogol exemplifies this theme in his "Diary of a Madman" (1835), which allows readers to follow the diarist-narrator's descent into madness. The theme is also prominent within Mikhail Lermontov's *A Hero of Our Time* (1840), Ivan Turgenev's "Diary of a Superfluous Man" (1850), and Fyodor Dostoevsky's *Notes from the Underground* (1864), three major works of Russian literature in which readers gain access to the psychological states of antihero protagonists through their diaristic self-narratives. The global influence of these texts can be seen in rewritings of the "mad diarist" motif in Lu Xun's "Diary of a Madman" (1918) and Junichiro Tanizaki's *Diary of a Mad Old Man* (1962).

The ability of the diary to represent the complexity of human experience explains the genre's significance within Modernist fiction. Increasingly throughout the twentieth century, the diary's fragmented structure was employed to mirror the fragmented nature of the modern world and to assert the fundamental inability of individuals to know or accurately represent themselves. In John-Paul Sartre's *Nausea* (1938), the protagonist's sickness is not the result of mental illness but of perceiving all too clearly the unstable nature of reality. Many other modernist works employ the diary form to foreground the unreliability of their narrators. Vladimir Nabokov's *Lolita* (1955) encloses the narrator's recalled-from-memory and heavily edited diary, which, although designed by the narrator to justify his pursuit of the prepubescent Lolita, calls into question the legitimacy of his version of events and the morality of his behavior. James Joyce concludes *A Portrait of the Artist as a Young Man* (1916) with an excerpt from his protagonist's diary that documents the gap between his grandiose artistic ambitions and the stasis of his life. And Julio Cortázar's short story "The Distances" (1951) employs a dramatic twist to undercut the reader's expectation that a diary is a reliable record of an individual's life by showing instead that individuals are composed of multiple, different, and antagonistic selves.

The use of the diary for the purpose of modernist experimentation is stretched even further within postmodern literature, in which the diary format enables a self-reflexive interrogation of the boundary line between fact and fiction, representation and reality, and self and other. While it is not possible here to provide a comprehensive overview of the many different works of diary fiction during the twentieth- and twenty-first centuries (some of which are explored elsewhere in this chapter), a few examples demonstrate the continued relevance of the form and its particular utility for addressing social issues. Percival Everett's *Erasure* (2001) confronts questions surrounding race and identity by juxtaposing two texts: A diary written by an African American academic and intellectual, and a novel written by the same man that employs exaggerated racial stereotypes. The narrator must grapple with the consequences when his novel is perceived as a more authentic representation of blackness than his actual life writing. George Saunders's "The Semplica Girl Diaries" (2013) presents a stinging critique of consumerism and exploitation in the form of a diary written by a well-meaning but oblivious everyman, who holds up a mirror for the reader to consider their own complicity in systems of global inequality. And, in the story "if a book is locked there's probably a good reason for that don't you think?" (2016), Helen Oyeyemi introduces magical realist elements into a story about race, gender, and office politics, employing a girlhood diary to show that the past exercises a mysterious but powerful hold over the present. These self-conscious and metatextual representations of the diary appear alongside an alternate trend in contemporary historical fiction, in which diaries are represented as material emblems of the past, in works such as A. S. Byatt's *Possession* (1990) and Sarah Waters's *Affinity* (1999).

This brief history highlights the place of diary fiction within canonical Western literature from the eighteenth century to the present. But this is not the whole story, as shown by early Japanese works like *The Tosa Diary* (c. 935) and *The Izumi Shikibu Diary* (c. 1005), which predate the emergence of diary fiction in the West.

Although the pages that follow document the proliferation of diary fiction across the globe in more recent years, a broader and more inclusive account of the history of fictional diaries in non-Western literary traditions remains to be written.

Resource: For a list of diary fiction, visit Henderson's *Diary Index*, www.diaryindex.com.

Reading Diary Fiction

The four conventions that I introduce here are designed to guide readers in their analysis of diary fiction. However, not all works of diary fiction will employ these devices and it is up to readers to decide whether or not they are relevant. The extent to which authors of diary fiction employ these conventions or develop entirely different ways of constructing their stories provide roadmaps for interpreting each story's meaning and significance.

Diary Manuscripts

Fictional diaries are almost always manuscript diaries. Although some works of diary fiction acknowledge the fact that diarists might compose their diaries on typewriters, computers, or digital devices, or record their diaries on audio devices or by using photographic, video, or other visual technologies, for the most part works of diary fiction represent diaries as handwritten manuscripts – paper artifacts that can be touched and handled by characters in the story. In fact, the materiality of the manuscript frequently functions as a key component of the story, in some cases taking precedence over the contents of the diary, which may or may not be shown to the reader. There is a particular interest in representing the diary manuscript's distinguishing marks or physical characteristics, such as the kind of notebook or paper used, or the quality of the diarist's handwriting. This attention to the surface of the diary is most pronounced in two recurring scenes: scenes of composition and scenes of discovery.

Scenes of composition portray the diarist in the act of writing, with an emphasis upon the materiality and embodied nature of diary writing. In George Orwell's *Nineteen Eighty-Four* (1949), the subversive nature of diary writing within an authoritarian society is conveyed through the textures and sensations of the writing instruments:

> [Winston] had procured [a pen], furtively and with some difficulty, simply because of a feeling that the beautiful creamy paper deserved to be written on with a real nib … He dipped the pen into the ink and then faltered for just a second … To mark the paper was the decisive act.
>
> (8)

In diary fiction written entirely in the form of a diary, this trope necessitates that diarists describe the mechanics of their writing to themselves, which may stretch the credulity of the reader. This attention to the details of writing also becomes, at times, the object of satire as in Sartre's *Nausea* when the narrator begins to describe his writing instruments ("here is a cardboard box holding my bottle of ink") only to abruptly break off, concluding "that's stupid, there's nothing I can say about it" (1).

Scenes of discovery, by contrast, portray someone other than the diarist coming into contact with the diary. The discovery of a diary may be the initiating action of the story or it may appear as a turning point in the plot. Both devices rely upon the reader's expectation that diaries hold transformative information that, when revealed, will drive the narrative forward. But, initially, the focus of these scenes is on the diary as object and the tantalizing secrets implied by its material existence. Jeff Vandermeer's science fiction novel *Annihilation* (2014) includes an uncanny scene of discovery after a scientist-explorer is sent into an otherworldly zone to investigate the disappearance of previous expeditions, and finds an enormous mound of discarded diaries – the records kept by previous explorers who never returned.

> The journals and other materials formed a moldering pile about twelve feet high and sixteen feet wide that in places

> near the bottom had clearly turned to compost, the paper rotting away … Torn pages, crushed pages, journal covers warped and damp.
>
> (111–12)

Vandermeer frustrates the reader's desire to access the diaries' contents (which are not reproduced within the novel) and instead uses the material condition of the diaries to convey the unknowability of the mysterious place and what transpired in the past. While many other scenes of discovery within diary fiction proceed to characters opening and turning the pages of a diary, Vandermeer and other authors share the perspective that the encounter with the diary as an object is sufficient to communicate with readers: to set a mood, to advance the plot, to foreshadow, and so forth.

The focus on the materiality of diary manuscripts also appears in many works of diary fiction through the attempt to reproduce the appearance of handwritten diaries within the typescript pages of print publications. Physically separating the dated heading from each diary entry and inserting blank lines between diary entries are common ways of making the reader feel like they are holding a diary manuscript in their hands, but many books also employ textual embellishments meant to mimic a handwritten document: fonts that resemble script, ornamental glyphs or other decorative devices, etc. Some works of diary fiction take these efforts to the extreme, such as Kenneth Patchen's *The Journal of Albion Moonlight* (1941) and James Merrill's *The (Diblos) Notebook* (1965), which use typographical variation, bold and italic typescript, crossed out and missing words, and other devices to evoke the appearance of a handwritten diary. As we will see, this interest in reproducing the appearance of manuscript diaries is pronounced in visual narrative forms like comic books and graphic novels, which have a greater capacity for accomplishing this goal. Despite the fact that print typography greatly limits what is possible in this respect, this recurring feature of diary fiction demonstrates that authors and publishers recognize the power of the diary as a visual symbol and seek to harness its expressive abilities.

However expressive, the fictional diary manuscript is also fragile. The very physical characteristics that make the diary seem precious or historic also indicate how easily it could be lost, damaged, or destroyed. Abbott describes this as the "topos of the threatened manuscript," writing "The drama of the survival of the text becomes a part of the drama of the text" (*Diary* 186–87). Ruth Ozeki's *A Tale for the Time Being* (2013) begins with a scene of discovery that also invokes the threat of destruction. A character named Ruth encounters a pile of garbage washed up on a Canadian beach, including a "scarred plastic freezer bag, encrusted with barnacles across its surface like a rash" (8). Inside the bag she finds a Hello Kitty lunchbox and inside that an assortment of documents including a book that is identified on its cover as a novel by Marcel Proust, but, when opened, is revealed to be a diary written by a Japanese girl named Nao. Ruth concludes that the diary was likely swept out to sea during the tsunami of 2011. Thus the story of its discovery is also an almost unbelievable story of survival, as the diary faced one of the most dangerous physical threats imaginable – one, it is supposed, that Nao did not herself survive – and managed to cross the Pacific Ocean intact. Although Ozeki places the diary under threat only to describe its incredible rescue, related images of water-logged, burnt, torn, moldy, dirty, damaged diaries – or ones threatened with physical damage – are frequent in diary fiction. The marks of age or destruction on the diary's surface contribute to the status of the text, testifying to its authenticity as a historical object or as a real diary. They also enhance the specialness of the reading experience. Readers of nonfiction diary manuscripts often feel that they have been granted a unique form of access because the text is singular or fragile. So too are readers of diary fiction encouraged to feel that the diary survived in order to be read by them.

These investments in the diary manuscript have the consequence of making manuscript characteristics available for manipulation in the form of parody, satire, or counterfeit. Authors rely on readers' preconceptions about diary manuscripts as precious, authentic objects and, at times, use them to fool or challenge their readers. Gillian Flynn's *Gone Girl* (2012) initially intermixes an account of an investigation into a missing woman's disappearance with passages from her diary that clearly point toward her husband as the culprit. Among the many twists in Flynn's mystery is the revelation that the diary is a fabrication, designed by the missing woman to frame her husband. A passage in the wife's first person voice informs us that she faked not only the confessional style of the diary, but the physical manuscript as well. She makes a point of writing with a variety of different pens and she partially burns the diary to make it look like her husband tried to destroy it (237, 356). The wife manipulates the diary's readers within the novel (the police), even as Flynn manipulates the novel's readers to initially place their trust in the diary passages. Both moves depend upon the reader's belief that diaries are trustworthy artifacts, whose formal qualities and material fragility constitute reliable clues about the history, meaning, and authenticity of the text.

Ultimately, the material presence of the diary manuscript within diary fiction creates an opportunity for authors to write about writing. Many scholars of diary fiction observe that "the theme of the [fictional] diary ... is the theme of writing a diary" (Prince 479). In essence, authors turn the focus onto themselves – or a fictional version of themselves – by using the diarist's writing practices or writing instruments to stand in for their own. At the same time, the descriptive detail given to the diary manuscript reflects the belief that manuscripts communicate through their form as well as through their contents. As we saw in Chapter 1, reading manuscripts and engaging with their visual or tactile characteristics is considered to be a specialized form of literacy. While fiction in standardized print form cannot fully reproduce the experience of reading a manuscript, diary fiction references and evokes that experience in order to serve the narrative's purposes.

- How does the story represent the material form or composition of the diary?
- What function does the diary as a material object play within the story?

- What ideas about writing or reading does the story present through its description of the diary manuscript and its composition, discovery, and/or destruction?

Diary Narrators

In most works of diary fiction, the narrator or protagonist is the diarist. This fact may appear self-evident but it introduces a key distinction between nonfiction and fictional diaries. Whereas in a nonfiction diary, the author and the diarist are the same (recall the convention of the *diary subject*), in a fictional diary, the author is different from the diarist. We understand that the diarist in a work of diary fiction is a fictional character, usually the narrator of the story or the *diarist-narrator*. Scholars observe that this results in a complicated narrative structure in which there appear to be two levels of storytelling: The diarist-narrator telling their own story through their diary, and the author telling the story of the diarist-narrator. Martens argues that this results in a "framed communicative situation" or a doubling of the familiar narrative triangle of author, subject, and reader (33). However, the nature of diary fiction blurs the distinction between the author and diarist because the diarist-narrator is also an author (the author of the diary) and, particularly in stories told entirely in diary form, the actual author can recede in significance and the fictional author (the diarist) can begin to seem like the true author of the text. Authors of diary fiction frequently exploit this feature in order to encourage readers to feel as if they are reading a nonfiction diary. Some works of diary fiction mask the fact that there is a distinct author by listing the diarist-narrator on the title page, such as in Doris Lessing's *The Diary of a Good Neighbor* (1983), which identified Jane Somers as the author. Others blur the distinction between author and diarist by representing the diarist as an author who is in the process of writing a novel, such as in André Gide's *The Counterfeiters* (1925), an effect Gide exaggerated by publishing the *Journal of The Counterfeiters* (1926), a diary account of writing the novel.

For the most part, authors of diary fiction employ the diary structure in order to create a sense of immediacy and interiority.

Readers are invited to suspend disbelief and embrace the pretense of direct access to the diarist-narrator's thoughts and feelings. There are other, common narrative devices that can accomplish similar results such as first person point of view, interior monologue, and stream of consciousness. Diary fiction shares some traits with these other styles of writing but takes advantage of popular ideas about diaries to heighten the reader's sense of privileged access. This effect is enhanced through the diarist-narrator's unique voice, which may be conveyed through the story's content (personal, self-disclosing, revealing of embarrassing or secret details) or through the story's diaristic style (abbreviated, fragmented, insular). Elizabeth Prentiss's *Stepping Heavenward* (1869) introduces the diarist-narrator through her own words in the first entry of her diary: "I meant to get up early this morning, but it looked dismally cold out of doors, and felt delightfully warm in bed. So I covered myself up, and made ever so many good resolutions" (7). The fact that the diarist openly admits her failures makes her sympathetic and facilitates the reader's sense of identification with her. It is as a result of techniques like these that diarist-narrators become such memorable characters, gaining passionate fans and imitators (as was the case with Prentiss's heroine). However, while the open and engaging voice of the diarist-narrator is a powerful feature of diary fiction, the use of the diary to organize or advance a story also introduces new narrative challenges.

First, the diarist-narrator must explain why they are writing. First person stories do not need to explain why the narrator is thinking because readers easily accept the pretense that they have been given access to the narrator's perspective for the duration of the story. But, the diarist-narrator is not just thinking or experiencing, they are documenting their thoughts and experiences, so authors often provide an explanation for why the diarist-narrator has turned to the diary as a mode of self-expression in this particular moment. Abbott identifies the most common explanation as the narrative of the cloistered writer. According to Abbott, diarist-narrators are "cloistered" or isolated from society, a situation which motivates them to begin to write a diary but which also means they write only for themselves ("Letters" 23).

This state of isolation may be literal: the title character of Defoe's *Robinson Crusoe* stranded on a deserted island; the narrator of John Fowles' *The Collector* (1963) held captive in a basement; the narrator of May Sarton's *As We Are Now* (1973) sent to a grim facility for the elderly, and so forth. Or the state of isolation may be figurative. In other words, the diarist-narrator may be responding to a sense of being cut off from society or denied freedom. For instance, the narrator of Teresa de la Parra's *Iphigenia* (1924) returns from France to the more conservative society of Venezuela, where she feels trapped by the restrictive gender norms imposed upon unmarried girls. She states, "I'm writing anything I please, because the paper, this white, shiny paper, lovingly keeps everything I tell it, and never, never is horrified, or fusses at me, or puts its hands over its ears" (112). Cloistered diarists write because the diary hears and sees them when no one else does, and because the diary provides them with a way to potentially communicate with the outside world.

Second, works of diary fiction typically explore how diary writing impacts the diarist-narrator. Diary fiction invites the reader to believe that the diarist-narrator's writing could potentially affect the unfolding narrative. Through the act of writing, the narrator reflects upon the events in their life, a process of self-discovery that can alter their actions or choices. (Of course, this is a fictional conceit because the author controls the narrative, not the diarist.) Once again Abbott provides a useful model for interpreting this aspect of diary fiction. He suggests that diary fiction can be divided into two kinds: Stories in which writing a diary has a positive effect upon the diarist-narrator, and stories in which it has a negative effect (*Diary* 48, 70). On the one hand, some works of diary fiction represent the diarist-narrator as learning from their experiences or developing as a character. In Wendy Guerra's *Everyone Leaves* (2006), the act of writing a diary enables the diarist-narrator to overcome the traumatic events of her early life including child abuse, political oppression, and heartbreak. On the other hand, some stories describe narrators who are incapable or unwilling to change, despite the self-reflective function of the diary. Abbott identifies Mikhail Lermontov's *A Hero of Our Time*

(1840) as exemplifying this negative effect. Although the diarist openly acknowledges his indifference towards others and his participation in acts of seduction and murder, it does not lead to self-improvement. Instead, the diary facilitates the diarist's destructive behavior and delusions. Patricia Highsmith's *Edith's Diary* (1977) follows this negative role to its extreme by portraying the diary as the direct cause of the title character's death. While Abbott infers a binary classification of positive and negative effects, readers of diary fiction may instead discover a mix of the two, as diarist-narrators struggle to overcome their flaws or grapple with the limits of their ability to change.

- How does the story characterize the diarist-narrator? In what ways does it seek to create a sense of identification between the diarist and the reader?
- What explanation is given regarding why the diarist-narrator writes? How does this shape your perception of the diarist or the text overall?
- How does the act of writing a diary impact the diarist-narrator: with positive, negative, or mixed effects?

Framing Narratives and the Editor-Reader

If authors of diary fiction are obligated to explain why the diarist-narrator writes, they are also often obligated to explain why the diary is available to be read. How is it that the reader is granted access to the diary? If the reader is to suspend disbelief and accept that the diary is real, then questions immediately gather regarding audience and publication. These questions are sparked by the conventional idea that nonfiction diaries are not supposed to be read by others. As discussed elsewhere in this book, reading someone else's diary can raise ethical concerns while, at the same time, diaries that openly seek or allow access to readers (especially through publication) may be interrogated for their truthfulness. These issues inform the representation of the diary within fictional texts. Many works of diary fiction employ a framing narrative to explain the diary's path to readers.

These usually take the form of a paratext, an introduction at the beginning of the story written from the perspective of an *editor-reader*. Ferdinand Oyono's *Houseboy* (1960) opens with a perilous nighttime journey through the jungle that concludes with the editor stating, "That was how I came to read Tonudi's diary" and explaining his choice to translate the diary and present it to "you," the reader (8). However, some authors innovate on this structure such as Chuck Palahniuk's *Diary* (2003), which encloses a letter at the end of the book that is addressed to Palahniuk by one of the novel's characters and gives him permission to publish the diary manuscript. In other works of diary fiction, the framing narrative takes on more prominence than the enclosed diary, becoming a full-fledged story in its own right while still fulfilling the role of the frame in terms of introducing, explaining, and justifying the presence of the diary in the text.

One of the most popular forms of the framing narrative is the *story of the found document*, about how the diary was found or discovered. As previously discussed, *scenes of discovery* are common in diary fiction and place emphasis upon the material form of the diary. When included in the framing narrative, such scenes of discovery are also designed to facilitate the reader's access to the text by providing an explanation for how the diary is available to be read. The story of the found document has two other useful functions: First, it establishes (or purports to establish) the authenticity of the diary. Diaries found under floorboards, beside deathbeds, or in bank vaults are invested with legitimacy as objects and, as a consequence, their contents are verified as truth. Second, the story of the found document insulates the diarist from the criticism that they sought to publicize their diary. If the diary was found and made public by another person, the diarist can preserve their status as someone who wrote for themselves alone. The story of the found document has been employed so often that it has become the object of satire. As Martens points out, even in the early history of diary fiction, "the convention of authentication was well on its way to becoming an ironic game" (63). She identifies Søren Kierkegaard's *Either/Or* (1843) as exemplifying this phenomenon. Kierkegaard parodies the familiar scene of discovery by portraying a character destroying a desk with a hatchet and inadvertently opening a hidden drawer containing a diary. The novel proceeds to deconstruct the authenticity of the diary through competing claims and denials regarding the diary's authorship, as well as through the introduction of several other, equally questionable diaries.

The explanatory framing narrative introduces an important character within diary fiction, the *editor-reader*. In many cases the first voice that the reader encounters in a work of diary fiction is not the diarist but the editor-reader, the individual who found the diary and who brings it to the public. In fact, Susan Gasster calls this character the "finder" (63). The presence of these two key characters – the diarist-narrator and the editor-reader – raises a question regarding which possesses the defining voice of the text. In some stories, the editor-reader is understood to be a subordinate figure, merely a vehicle for granting the reader access to the diary. In other stories, the editor-reader has a more significant role, functioning as a second narrator or co-protagonist whose voice and perspective takes precedence within the text. The hyphenated term *editor-reader* references this character's two roles. The character is frequently the diary's editor, shaping the diary that is before us through typical editorial acts: transcribing, translating, annotating, rearranging, or expurgating the text. In this sense, the character is a fictional counterpart to the editors of nonfiction diaries discussed in Chapter 2. Novels like Siri Hustvedt's *The Blazing World* (2014) explicitly mimic the editorial apparatus of a critical edition of a diary, including an editor's introduction, interviews with experts, and footnotes. Sometimes the editor's role is transparent and reliable but, at other times, the editor's alterations to or control of the text raise suspicions regarding the final product. Edited diaries, even fictional ones, may be mediated diaries, involving a power differential between editor and diarist that requires readers to pay careful attention to how the editor is shaping the diary's content. At the same time, the editor-reader is also a reader: They are often the first person to read the diary after the diarist and the meaning of the diary is conveyed in part through the editor-reader's response to the text. This contributes to the complex structure of diary fiction. The reader is invited to identify with the diarist-narrator but they may also experience a competing draw to identify with the editor-reader, whose experience of reading the diary mirrors the reader's own.

The presence of an editor-reader and other characters can transform a work of diary fiction from a strict first person point of view into a multi-vocal, multi-perspective story. While a story entirely in the form of a diary is restricted to the diarist's perspective and understanding of events, the introduction of other voices can be a useful device for complicating the diary narration, particularly to include information that would not be available to the diarist. The editor-reader is a prominent means of crafting a second voice but several other techniques are possible. Diarists might copy someone else's writing into their diaries; the diarist might record conversations with other characters; another character might annotate or insert their own entries into the diary, and so forth. At times the second voice takes a surprising form such as in Eliza Jane Cate's "Susy L—'s Diary" (1849–1850), in which the diarist begins to engage in a dialog with a fairy in the pages of her diary. The fairy appears to know more about the diarist's life than the diarist herself, although the reader is also invited to understand the fairy interlocutor is a creation of the diarist. While the goal of such devices is to free the reader from the limited perspective of the diarist, it can also have the effect of revealing the diarist's blind spots. As Martens states, "it [is] exceptionally easy for an author to present a deluded or 'unreliable' narrator – one whose insights are undermined by a dissenting second voice" (37). Again, this complicates the reader's identification with the diarist by placing the reader in the position to judge the diarist's insight or choices, and perhaps to conclude that the diarist's version of events is flawed or deluded. Overall, diary fiction is deeply interested in the experience of diary reading, often modeling the effects (positive and negative) on people who read diaries, and making diary reading itself a galvanizing component of the plot.

- What is the story's framing narrative? What voices or perspectives does it introduce into the text?

- What role does the editor-reader play in the text? How does this character shape the reader's own experience?
- If the story does not employ a framing narrative and/or editor-reader, how does it address the question of why the diary is available to be read?

Diary Time and the Problem of Plot

Nonfiction diaries are characterized by their chronological structure, demarcated by sequential dated headings, and by their focus on representing the present moment or the "middleness" of experience. These defining features, introduced in Chapter 3, are what give nonfiction diaries a sense of immediacy and vitality – but they also present problems for authors of fiction, which is typically organized by a plot. Diaries are usually described as plot-less because the lives of ordinary people are unpredictable, unstructured, and often un-dramatic. How do authors compose a plotted story with conventions like rising action, climax, and denouement while preserving the diary's recognizable temporal structure? Moreover, because diarists are in the middle of their stories and cannot predict the future, stories in diary form cannot easily employ foreshadowing or plant meaningful symbols. How can authors overcome the narrative limitations of the diary in order to make due without – or to create new ways of expressing – foreshadow, symbolism, or other familiar storytelling methods?

Many works of diary fiction strive to mimic the characteristics of diary time despite the requirements of plot. Most employ dated headings to signal the passage of time. In fact, the presence of a dated heading is often the first clue that readers encounter to indicate that they are reading a work of diary fiction. The date effectively places the reader within the fictional experience of diary reading. The dated structure allows authors to exploit the feeling that diaries possess of representing experiences as they are occurring, what is known as "intercalated narration," when the events of the story and their representation in the diary appear to alternate (Rimmon-Kenan 90). This has the effect of "clos[ing] the gap between the time of the narrating and the time of the narrated" (Abbott, *Diary* 189). The techniques writers employ to close the gap between action and description of action at times require readers to suspend disbelief such as in Stoker's *Dracula*, when characters who are fleeing for their lives pause to describe their experiences in their diaries. This emphasis upon the immediacy of the narrated story corresponds to the nonretrospective nature of nonfiction diaries. Like the diary itself, many fictional diaries document events in the present tense and as they happen, instead of looking back from a point in the future. Some diary stories reject the nonretrospective structure and instead represent diaries that are specifically designed to tell a story from the diarist's past. In Iris Murdoch's *The Sea, The Sea* (1978), the diarist-narrator begins keeping a present tense diary but soon dispenses with dated headings and starts to describe his childhood, and before long the boundaries between past, present, and future have irrevocably blurred. For the most part, however, the chronological and nonretrospective fictional diary serves to heighten suspense by placing the reader alongside the diarist in the middle of experience and in a state of ignorance about the future.

While diary fiction mimics some aspects of diary time, it typically does not adopt this convention exactly because readers are not likely to find an exhaustive daily record of a character's life entertaining. Mark Twain satirizes the tediousness of the diary in a fictional snapshot of his childhood diary in *The Innocents Abroad* (1869) writing, "Monday – Got up, washed, went to bed. Tuesday – Got up, washed, went to bed. Wednesday – Got up, washed, went to bed," and so forth (508–9). Storytellers strive to avoid such repetitiveness and instead to emphasize the plot that underlies the chronological structure of the diary. In Andrew Hassam's words, "diary novels have upon them the responsibility of the novel to give meaning to the series of daily events that have apparently occurred fortuitously" (*Writing* 39). In order to accomplish this goal, authors of diary fiction employ a variety of techniques. The previously discussed devices of the frame narrative and the introduction of additional characters' voices are two mechanisms for developing a story's plot. In addition, many fictional diaries are acknowledged as edited texts, with the boring or un-plotted parts of the diary omitted. As the editor-reader in Boualem Sansal's *The German Mujahid* (2008) states, "I've cut out a lot of stuff and kept the best bits" (35). Authors also employ interruptions in diarists' writing to omit uninteresting aspects of their lives (leaping over days when nothing important happens, for example), as well as to vary the rhythm of the text in order to speed up or slow down narrative momentum. And very frequently, works of diary fiction are indistinguishable from stories using first person narration. These texts give up the pretense that they are diaries in order to take advantage of more conventional and flexible storytelling modes.

The adaptation of diary time draws particular attention to two important moments within the fictional diary, beginnings and endings. Frame narratives provide one kind of beginning by recounting how the diary was set on the path that lead to it being available to readers. Many works of diary fiction also emphasize the circumstances that motivate the diarist to begin writing, typically external motivations that correlate closely with the catalyst for the story itself: conflict, discovery, new experiences or challenges, or urgent needs or desires. These motivations may parallel those that drive actual diarists to begin writing, spelled out in the declarations of purpose common at the beginning of nonfiction diaries. Only rarely do fictional diarists indicate that they have been keeping a diary before the action of the story begins because this fact can cause the story to feel incomplete; after all, why would the reader be limited to only a portion of the fictional diary? A fictional diarist's motivation for beginning a diary is among the first clues the author provides regarding the narrator's character and circumstances, and are therefore worth analyzing closely. Endings, on the other hand, prove as challenging in fictional diaries as they are in nonfiction diaries. Neither form has a natural or inevitable endpoint. As a result, readers of diary fiction may question why the story ends here and now. Some endings are awkward and unsatisfying, unable to adequately justify the conclusion of the narrative, given the structuring device of the diary. Other works of diary fiction employ the ending of the text to paint a final, revealing portrait of the diarist's state of the mind or their life circumstances. Often, the cessation in writing has pessimistic overtones: a complete breakdown, a silencing of the diarist's voice, or the diarist's death. At other times, the cessation in writing might be interpreted more optimistically: a challenge overcome, freedom acquired, or the diarist moving on to new and better things.

There are some important exceptions to these general characteristics, works of diary fiction that fundamentally reimagine the temporal structure of the nonfiction diary. Many writers reject the chronological sequence of dated diary entries in favor of innovative organizational systems. Michel Laub's *Diary of the Fall* (2011) is composed of a series of sequentially numbered paragraphs, a technique that creates a sense of forward momentum through the short and tightly-linked paragraphs, while also conveying the idea that time is recursive or repetitive. This structure reflects the novel's central meditation on the parallels between the Holocaust and the high school experiences of a Holocaust survivor's grandson. In Laub's novel, the diary form is not designed to impose a linear order on time but to expose the instability of past and present.

- What aspects of diary time does the story preserve and what aspects does it alter or adapt, and why?
- Identify key moments in the story when the temporal structure of the narration is important, and explore the significance.

Major Themes and Intersecting Genres

As this chapter indicates, diary fiction has a long history and has played a significant role across world literature. The body of writing that can be classified as diary fiction is enormous, diverse, and still growing. The themes and related genres identified here are designed to help readers by organizing some of these works into clusters around similar topics or modes of representation. The fact that these texts make use of the diary puts them in conversation with each other, despite their different time periods or national literary traditions. However, it will be clear that the themes and intersecting genres identified here provide only a few, specific ways of thinking about these texts and readers are encouraged to explore alternate critical lenses as well.

Gender, Sex, and Sexuality

Two influential ideas about the nonfiction diary contribute to the fact that many works of diary fiction are centrally concerned with the representation of gender, sex, and sexuality: The perception of the diary as a feminine form of writing and the belief that diaries are private. Although elsewhere in this book I have proposed that these two ideas deserve to be reexamined, it is worth exploring how they have been taken up within fictional texts. For many authors, the fact that diaries are associated with femininity and domesticity creates an opportunity to use the diary form to represent women's experiences. Authors take advantage of the feminization of the genre in order to legitimate their focus on women and to develop unique female voices. At the same time, the fact that diaries are thought to be repositories for private or intimate experiences creates an opportunity for authors to use the diary form to represent sex and sexuality, including the LGBTQIA experience. Some works of diary fiction simply replicate conventional ideas or clichés about women, privacy, and the diary but many others take up these conventions in order to construct new ways of understanding gender, sex, and sexuality. Indeed, many of these texts express feminist and/or queer perspectives, employing the diary to articulate a critique of heteropatriarchy.

Questions for exploring gender, sex, and sexuality in diary fiction:

- Why does the author use the diary in order to address the themes of gender, sex, and/or sexuality in the story?
- Does using the diary to write about women's experiences reinforce or challenge stereotypical associations between women and domesticity, interiority, emotions, and privacy?
- How does the feminization of the diary impact diary fiction about male-authored diaries or stories in which masculinity is a pronounced theme?

- Does the representation of sex or sexuality reinforce the perception that these are private, individual, or even shameful matters, or does it offer new ways of understanding them?
- In what ways does the diary allow authors to explore nonbinary conceptions of gender and sexuality?

Recommended Reading:

Anita Loos, *Gentlemen Prefer Blondes* (1925)
Ding Ling, "Miss Sophia's Diary" (1927)
Mario Benedetti, *The Truce* (1960)
Junichiro Tanizaki, *The Key* (1961)
Doris Lessing, *The Golden Notebook* (1962)
Simone de Beauvoir, *The Woman Destroyed* (1967)
Zhang Jie, "Love Must Not Be Forgotten" (1979)
Alice Walker, *The Color Purple* (1982)
Hervé Guibert, *To the Friend Who Did Not Save My Life* (1990)
Qiu Miaojin, *Notes of a Crocodile* (1994)
Helen Fielding, *Bridget Jones's Diary* (1996)
Xiaolu Guo, *A Concise Chinese-English Dictionary for Lovers* (2007)

Colonialism and Postcolonialism

The nonfiction diary played a formative role in Western colonialism in both abstract and concrete ways. The perception of the diary as a form of Western writing, although a contested view, created an association between diary writing and Western individualism and literacy. Historically, many Europeans and Americans wrote diary accounts of their experiences as colonizers, using their autobiographical narratives to justify their authority over colonial subjects. Many of these diaries were published, shaping the popular perception of "the other" in the West and reinforcing systems of power and exploitation. These facts create an opportunity for contemporary authors to use the diary structure for fictional accounts of colonial and postcolonial experiences. For the most part, authors critical of colonialism adopt the diary in order to subvert its association with Euro-American cultural supremacy and to assert the subjectivity and selfhood of colonized people. Many also present Western colonialism and heteropatriarchy as related systems of oppression, linking this theme with the one discussed earlier.

Questions for exploring colonialism and postcolonialism in diary fiction:

- How does the story address or respond to the perception of the diary as a "white" or Western form of writing?
- Is the diary format adapted to give voice to non-Western characters or world views? If so, in what ways? If not, what are the implications?
- In what ways are colonial power relations replicated or critiqued within the story?
- What options or alternatives, if any, does the story present for reshaping the political structure of colonial or postcolonial society?

Recommended Reading:

Mongo Beti, *The Poor Christ of Bomba* (1956)
Ferdinand Oyono, *Houseboy* (1960)
Myriam Warner-Vieyra, *Juletane* (1982)
Mia Couto, *Sleepwalking Land* (1992)
Ahmadou Kourouma, *Allah Is Not Obliged* (2000)
David Mitchell, *Cloud Atlas* (2004)
J. M. Coetzee, *Diary of a Bad Year* (2007)
Boualem Sansal, *The German Mujahid* (2009)

Young Adult Fiction

Many people associate diary writing with young adulthood, viewing the practice as one that will help young people survive the challenges of adolescence. This idea explains why so many works of young adult or YA fiction take diary form. The modern practice of linking the diary and the coming-of-age experience has been attributed to the prevalence of Anne Frank's diary on schoolchildren's reading lists (Pinsent), as well as to cultural anxieties regarding the need for young people to develop healthy interpersonal relationships (Day). A defining feature of YA diary fiction is the strong narrative voice of the diarist. Very often this voice is light-hearted and exuberant, fostering a sense of identification between young readers and the diarist-narrator. Yet, the humorous style also allows authors to address complex personal and social issues. In many cases it is the unsentimental and uncensored diaristic voice that facilitates the story's political critique. Numerous YA diary novels are written in the form of historical diaries, mimicking them so effectively that young readers can be led to believe they are reading an authentic nonfiction diary. Others employ the intimate and interior style of the diary to enable readers to witness trauma, violence, or other horrors alongside the diarist-narrator. And many works of YA diary fiction make extensive use of visual images or are written in the form of graphic novels or memoirs, linking them to the subsequent theme of graphic narrative.

Questions for exploring young adult diary fiction:

- Why is the diary form useful for granting the reader access to a young protagonist's story? Why might it be particularly effective at reaching a young reading audience?
- What role does diary writing have for the protagonist as they navigate the challenges of coming-of-age?
- To what extent does the story adopt or adapt conventional ideas about diaries, such as the feminization of the genre, its purported privacy, or its historical accuracy? How do these choices relate to the overarching meaning or message of the text?
- What visual or stylistic techniques does the story employ to replicate the structure or appearance of a diary?
- Many works of YA diary fiction are published as book series or have been successfully adapted to serial media forms like

television and film? Why? What makes the diary compatible to serialized fiction? What can these adaptations teach us about the diary in popular culture?

Recommended Reading:

Dodie Smith, *I Capture the Castle* (1948)
Sue Townsend, *The Secret Diary of Adrian Mole, Aged 13 ¾* (1982)
Dear America series (1996–), see also related series: *My Name is America*, *Dear Canada*, *Darios Mexicanos*, and *Mon Histoire*, etc.
Stephen Chbosky, *The Perks of Being a Wallflower* (1999)
Meg Cabot, *The Princess Diaries* (2000)
George O'Connor, *Journey into Mohawk Country* (2006)
Sherman Alexie, *The Absolutely True Diary of a Part-Time Indian* (2007)
Jeff Kinney, *Diary of Wimpy Kid* (2007)
Claudia Mills, *The Totally Made-up Civil War Diary of Amanda MacLeish* (2008)
Rachel Renée Russell, *Dork Diaries: Tales From a Not-So-Fabulous Life* (2009)
L. J. Smith, *The Vampire Diaries* (2010)
Mariko Tamaki and Jillian Tamaki, *Skim* (2010)
Jerdine Nolen, *Eliza's Freedom Road: An Underground Railroad Diary* (2011)
Keshni Kashyap, *Tina's Mouth: An Existential Comic Diary* (2012)
Isabel Quintero, *Gabi: A Girl in Pieces* (2014)
Veera Hiranandani, *The Night Diary* (2018)

Comics, Graphic Novels, and Graphic Memoir

Diaries are common devices within comics, graphic novels, and graphic memoir. Although these genres are very different in terms of history, audience, status as literary texts, and claim to truthfulness, for the purpose of this brief introduction I will discuss them as related forms of graphic narrative. Two major issues come to the forefront when considering how and why diaries are represented within graphic narrative. First, graphic narrative gives authors the ability to visually reproduce a diary or handwritten diary page, highlighting the theme of the material manuscript. Second, the representation of time in nonfiction diaries shares some notable parallels with the way that time is represented within graphic narrative: as segmented, sequential, divided by gaps or white spaces, etc. The diary form invites a close examination of the sequences, rhythms, spaces, and visual effects that create a sense of time within graphic texts. Diary comics are a specific kind of graphic narrative, consisting of daily accounts of ordinary life written in comic form. Diaries also appear within graphic novels and memoirs as objects or intertexts. In graphic memoirs, the diary is often designed to highlight the tensions between memory, truth, and self-representation that characterize autobiography. While the diary is sometimes used to authenticate the author's version of events, it is equally called upon to communicate the impossibility of recording experience, past or present (Figure 4.1). Many works of graphic diary fiction also focus on female sexuality, reinforcing the theme of gender, sex, and sexuality. The diary format enables authors to grapple with challenging and controversial subjects like sexual abuse, rape, coming out, nonbinary gender identity, and other issues.

Questions for exploring the diary in graphic narrative:

- Is the function of a diary altered if it takes graphic instead of verbal form? Why and in what ways?
- What visual or other representational techniques does the story employ to replicate the structure or appearance of the diary?
- How does the diary influence the visual or temporal form of the graphic narrative?
- What ideas about memory and self-representation is the diary employed to represent or explore within the narrative?

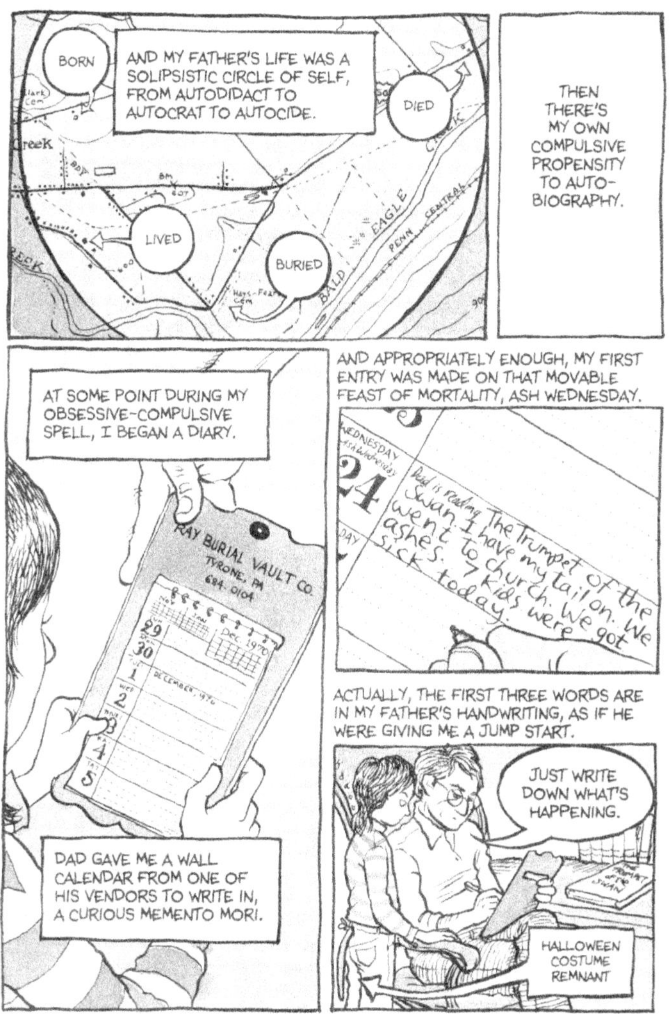

Figure 4.1 Page 140 from *Fun Home: A Family Tragicomic* by Alison Bechdel. Copyright © 2006 by Alison Bechdel. Used by permission of Houghton Mifflin Harcourt Publishing Company. All rights reserved

Recommended Reading:

- Lewis Trondheim, *Little Nothings* (1993–)
- James Kochalka, *American Elf* (1998–2012)
- Phoebe Gloeckner, *The Diary of a Teenage Girl* (2002)
- Erika Moen, *DAR! A Super Girly Top Secret Comic Diary* (2003–2009)
- Alison Bechdel, *Fun Home* (2006)
- Julie Morah, *Blue is the Warmest Color* (2010)
- Dustin Harbin, *Diary Comics* (2012–)
- Gabrielle Bell, *Truth is Fragmentary* (2014)
- Barroux, *Line of Fire: Diary of an Unknown Soldier* (2014)
- Emil Feris, *My Favorite Thing is Monsters* (2016)
- Pam Smy, *Thornhill* (2017)
- Anne Frank, *Anne Frank's Diary: The Graphic Adaptation* (2018)

Fiction in the Nonfiction Diary

It makes sense to think of diary fiction as being inspired by nonfiction diaries. Nonfiction diaries historically predate their earliest fictional counterparts and many works of diary fiction are clearly written in response to well-known or historically important nonfiction diaries. However, it can also prove useful to explore the opposite trajectory of influence and consider how diary fiction, and fiction more generally, shape nonfiction diaries. As Steven Kagle and Lorenza Gramegna state, the relationship between nonfiction and fictional diaries "is not unidirectional. Just as a diary may inspire and direct fiction, so fiction and its patterns may inspire and direct a diary" (38). This chapter has shown the prevalence of diary fiction across a long literary history and in many different national traditions and languages. As soon as these works of diary fiction began to be published, it became possible for readers to learn about the diary from fictional diaries. Many diarists encounter the diary for the first time by reading diary fiction and model their diary writing on what they see in these works. At the same time, many diarists employ fictional devices in their diaries, mimicking the style or language of authors they admire or using their diaries to develop authorial voices of their own. Although this blurring of fact and fiction may appear to some to be contradictory to the expected function of the diary as a truthful record of the self, fictionalization deserves to be explored as a legitimate component of autobiographical self-narrative. The popularity of diary fiction across the globe calls upon readers to attend to how fictional texts have and continue to produce new generations of diarists.

Essential Question #4: Are Diaries More Truthful than Other Forms of Writing?

Would your diary pass a historical accuracy test? In 1921, W. N. P. Barbellion's diary was subjected to such a test by historian A. F. Pollard, who compared Barbellion's diary to meteorological and military records, found discrepancies with his version of events, and concluded that as a result the diary fails as a diary. "When is a diary not a diary? Obviously when it gets hopelessly mixed in the days of the week and anticipates events by months" (Pollard 27). H. R. Cummings (Barbellion's brother) defended his brother's diary from "the big stick called the 'historical method'" wielded by Pollard, but Pollard remained intransigent and insisted that "the evidentiary value of documents, purporting to be diaries, could be tested" and discrepancies were "fatal to the value of these diaries as historical evidence" (Cummings 188, 193). While Pollard's nitpicking over differing accounts of the weather may appear extreme, many readers share his expectation that diaries should be factually truthful, especially if they are to have historical value.

The perception of diaries as truthful records is linked to their status as original manuscripts, as private or unpublished forms of writing, and as having and seeking no readers – all issues that are explored elsewhere in this book. Despite the complexity of these issues, the association between diary writing and truth is pervasive and influential. William Matthews states, "To the historian, the cardinal value of the good diary is perhaps its realism" ("Diary as History" cxvi). But even when read as literary rather than historical texts, diaries are judged by what Robert Fothergill calls "the spontaneous-sincerity school of thought" (47). This is the idea that the literary characteristics of the diary (its artlessness and immediacy) testify to the authenticity of the diary's contents and, therefore, to its truthful representation of the diary self.

Yet, many others find the idea of measuring a diary for its truthfulness to be a flawed endeavor. Lawrence Rosenwald asserts, "To assert that journal accounts are governed only by the uncontaminated expressive impulses of the writer is false because it is impossible" (22). Within the field of autobiography studies, scholars concur that the expectation that any self-writing is or should be a truthful representation of the writer is an impossible standard. Instead, scholars argue, autobiography must be understood as a form of writing with as much in common with fiction, and even with lies, as with truth. John Paul Eakin declares, "autobiographical truth is not a fixed but an evolving content in an intricate process of self-discovery and self-creation, and … the self that is the center of all autobiographical narrative is necessarily a fictive structure" (*Fictions* 3). Timothy Dow Adams describes this alternate conception of truth as "narrative truth" (12) while Sidonie Smith and Julia Watson term it "intersubjective truth" (16). Diary scholars agree with these reconsiderations of truth, arguing that diaries deserve to be understood as, in Elizabeth Hampsten's words, "true to life" but not necessarily "true to fact" (15). In other words, diarists represent a version of their life and times that reflects their truth, whether or not it measures neatly against other documentary evidence.

For diarists, a flexible notion of truth provides opportunities for self-expression that a strict adherence to fact would not allow. Anaïs Nin wrote to her diary, "You and I waging our great battle for truth, secretly and quietly, but our purpose is not to describe Anaïs Nin; indeed not – what a waste of time that would be" (January 20, 1922). While Nin's truth emerges through her rejection of a coherent diary self, for other diarists, the departure from truth is the means by which they convey a sense of self. Cesare Pavese (Italian, 1908–1950) states, "What I say may not be true, but the fact that I say it betrays my inner being" (October 27, 1946). And, in an essay on her lifelong practice of keeping notebooks, Joan Didion (American, 1934–) writes that her goal "has never been … to have an accurate factual record of what I have been doing or thinking" but to "[r]emember what it was to be me," a personal and individualistic standard of truth (133, 136).

Such broad conceptions of truth may be liberating for diarists but they often create discomfort for readers. Adams writes that readers are left with an "uneasy feeling" regarding whether or not they are allowed to expect accuracy in autobiographical writing (12). Famous diary hoaxes like the Hitler diaries in the 1980s or the more recent *A Gay Girl in Damascus* blog hoax demonstrate why it remains necessary to distinguish between diaries that employ narrative or intersubjective truth, and those that are entirely fabricated. The fact that Holocaust deniers have launched an extended campaign claiming that Anne Frank's diary is fake indicates what is at stake in the act of labeling diaries as truth or fiction.

Are diaries more truthful than other forms of writing? It would be more accurate to say that diaries present truths about the diarist or the diarist's own perception of truth, without necessarily fulfilling an ideal of historical fidelity. Coming to terms with the diarist's own standards regarding accuracy, and their use of fact, fiction, or even lies as modes of self-expression will assist readers in gaining a better understanding of the diarist and their writing.

5 Reading Digital Diaries

The history of the diary demonstrates the genre's capacity to evolve in response to technological changes that impact writing and self-representation. Although diaries were originally composed using pen and paper, diarists began typing their diaries as soon as the typewriter was developed. Today diarists write their diaries on personal computers and increasingly employ digital tools including online programs and hand-held devices. In fact, the list of platforms or devices that have been identified as or compared to diaries is extensive and includes: social media networks like Facebook, Twitter, Instagram, and Pinterest; movement trackers, including wearable cameras or audio recording devices; geolocation tools; text message, direct message, or phone records; emails; online calendars; health, fitness, and productivity apps like calorie counters or period trackers; web browser histories; streaming video, TV, or movie viewing histories; digital photographic records; video game play logs, including audio and video recordings, and so forth. As this list indicates, it can start to seem as if everything done on or with a computer is a diary, whether we recognize it or not. Kathryn Carter writes, "we are all *de facto* diarists, at least those of us who have online access and presence" (428). At the same time, many of the features of digital diary writing appear to challenge the characteristics that have long been thought to define the genre, especially when self-narratives are posted online or when diary-like data is collected about an individual without their knowledge or consent.

This chapter examines digital diaries, a loosely connected body of written material that falls into three general categories: First, writing that self-consciously styles itself as modern or computer-generated equivalents to pen-and-paper diaries, such as blogs, vlogs, diary apps, or online diary writing programs. Second, forms of digital self-representation that are not explicitly modeled on the diary but which nevertheless perform tasks traditionally fulfilled by diaries, including social media accounts, text messages, and smartphone photographs that record daily life, reveal personal details, and preserve memories. Texts such as these raise challenging questions regarding whether a text can be considered a diary if the author did not think of themselves as writing a diary. Third, the digital data that an individual generates through their online activity but which is collected by a third party and that may be inaccessible to the individual. This data may document the daily activities and interests of an individual on a very intimate level, but can it be legitimately identified as a diary? This chapter explores all three kinds of self-writing or self-documentation and how they extend and complicate the diary genre. I consider how four key concepts discussed elsewhere in this book with reference to traditional diaries are adapted or reimagined within digital environments: manuscripts, diary subjects, privacy and diary readers, and diary time. I conclude the chapter by proposing that reading digital diaries can teach us important lessons regarding traditional diaries, including ways to think anew about privacy, collaboration, and multimodality across diary history.

Is It a Diary if It's Online?

This chapter focuses on digital diaries, which are diaries or diary-like texts that are born digital, originating through computer software or digital devices. In comparison to the *digitized diaries* discussed in Chapter 2, *digital diaries* rely upon computers for their creation, the keyboard and the screen filling the roles historically played by pen and paper (Figure 5.1). Although the technology of composition, preservation, circulation, and reproduction has greatly changed, the link between handwritten or

Figure 5.1 Promotional advertisement for Momento, a diary app launched in 2010. © 2018 d3i Ltd. Used by permission from d3i Ltd

analog diaries and digital diaries deserves to be acknowledged and explored. However, the nature of that link is subject to debate. When scholars think about the relationship between old and new media, and particularly about traditional genres like diaries in comparison to digital forms like blogs or social media, they characterize that relationship in several, distinct ways. Some argue that new media has no relationship to the past. Daniel Punday summarizes this view, writing that "cybertexts … are like some new species recently discovered: any attempt to impose traditional textual categories from other media … is by definition a misinterpretation of the form" (19). For this reason, some scholars argue that even those online formats that appear to mimic diaries should not be interpreted as diaries. For instance, addressing the question of whether blogs are modern equivalents to diaries, Julie Rak states, "weblogs are not a continuation of diary writing in a new form. Weblogs are better understood as an internet genre with a history as long as the history of the internet itself" (170).

By contrast, some scholars characterize the relationship between old and new media as exhibiting the growth or evolution of human communication, with new media replacing old because it possesses superior capabilities. Following this argument, scholars emphasize the "affordances" (new tools or properties) that online diaries possess and which enable diarists to express themselves more fully or with greater immediacy than was possible with paper diaries. Yet, the evolutionary model has also been criticized as a form of "technological determinism" that establishes a hierarchical value system in which new media is viewed as unquestionably better than what it replaces (Kitzmann, "Different" 58). Finally, scholars describe the relationship between old and new media as one of "remediation," a term that refers to the ways in which new media reuses and refashions preexisting forms, and as a result remains dependent upon old media for inspiration and structure (Bolter and Grusin). This model acknowledges that traditional media is important to digital formats, even though it may be altered by technological affordances. For example, Susan Herring et al. argue that "blogs are neither unique nor reproduced entirely from offline genres, but rather constitute a hybrid genre that draws from multiple sources, including other internet communication genres" (144). It is this third model that informs my analysis of digital diaries in this chapter. Rather than viewing digital diaries as simple reproductions of analog diaries or considering them to be completely distinct genres, I emphasize the middle ground of dialog, influence, and adaptation. Historicizing digital diaries in this way presents an opportunity to rethink the meanings and values associated with "old" and "new" media, particularly given the long history of the diary genre as a changing and adaptable literary form.

In addition to debating the relationship between old and new media, scholars also debate whether it makes sense to apply traditional genre classifications to online materials. As we have seen throughout this book, defining genres and deciding where and how to apply these definitions are major components of literary analysis, and ones that carry over to the analysis of digital texts. Some scholars question whether an old-fashioned genre category like the diary has any relevance to the kinds of autobiographical writing that occurs online or on digital devices. But others believe that genre studies remains a valuable resource for interpreting digital texts, even though they argue we must acknowledge the specific attributes of the electronic medium. Inger Askehave and Anne Ellerup Nielsen state, "although many web genres have printed counterparts … the medium adds unique properties to the web genre," properties that "cannot be ignored in the genre characterization" (125). Scholars find further evidence of the importance of genre in digital environments in the fact that so many authors describe their online writing with reference to predigital genres. In some cases, the goal is to distance the analog and the digital. Laurie McNeill observes that many bloggers employ a "negative definition" along the lines of "this blog is *not* a diary," a move that she attributes in part to the negative gender stereotypes associated with the diary ("Brave" 145, 148). In other cases, the goal is to cement the association between analog and digital. Kylie Cardell writes about digital texts that "self-nominate" as diaries through title, format, style, or voice in order to take advantage of readers' assumptions about the authenticity or truthfulness of diaries (*Dear* 98). For many online authors, the diary genre remains a touchstone that informs their choices regarding whether or how to share their personal writing on the web. For this reason, the conventions of the traditional diary remain useful interpretative tools for readers exploring the form and content of digital diaries.

Reading Digital Diaries

Reading digital diaries through the lens of the traditional diary involves revisiting many of the major terms and concepts that define the diary, but which take on new meaning within the context of digital media. Placing these "new" diaries in a lineage with "old" diaries establishes a historical framework through which to examine the influence of established ideas and practices upon innovative modes of self-representation. At the same time, foregrounding the changes that digital formats bring to the diary, and which in many cases appear to fundamentally alter the form and function of the genre, allows readers to explore the ongoing development of the genre.

Manuscripts and Digital Materiality

Diaries do not always take manuscript form but the idea of the diary as a handwritten paper document is pervasive, even in digital formats. Although digital diaries may appear antithetical to diary manuscripts because they are electronic and intangible, in fact material manuscripts remain important influences upon the construction, reception, and use of digital diaries.

The phrase "digital materiality" refers to the idea that even digital texts have dimension, shape, and structure. While you cannot touch or handle a diary written with an online diary program, it does have a quasi-material form created by the hardware used to write or access it and by the choices the author has made in terms of how their online diary is formatted, illustrated, or networked. Just as scholars advocate that readers should attend to the choices diarists make when they compose a diary manuscript, they also recognize the importance of examining the choices digital diarists make when they design a website, personalize an account, and so forth. These design choices can be understood to constitute a mode of communicative expression. Madeleine Sorapure writes, "The notion of writing is thus redefined for online diarists, as they also 'write' with images, navigation choices, and site structure" (5). In fact, José van Dijck argues that the ways that diarists individualize their online identities functions as kind of digital signature, comparable to a writer's unique style of handwriting (65–66). Cardell goes so far as to state that digital diaries are "closer to a manuscript than any other format" because both writing technologies (pen and paper; keyboard and screen) allow for flexibility, openness, and multiplicity (*Dear* 114). However, McNeill cautions that many kinds of software and online interfaces limit how much writers can express their individuality, stating that use of these technologies requires "submission of the human subject to the software's imperatives," such dropdown fields, preset options, and restricted formats ("There" 268). The tension between the freedom of self-expression made possible by Web 2.0 technology and the limits these formats impose upon users is a defining characteristic of digital life writing.

One topic that complicates the comparison of manuscript and digital materiality is the question of permanence and/or impermanence, and the shifting nature of these terms. Many think of paper manuscripts as possessing greater longevity than online materials, which are perceived as ephemeral and unstable. Others reverse these values, viewing paper materials as easily lost or destroyed, whereas digital records are reliable and enduring. Read through these different evaluative concepts, digital diaries are claimed as both more and less "material" than paper diaries. Further complicating these designations is the fact that diaries sometimes switch mediums. Lee Humphreys describes the act of converting a digital text into a paper object as "rematerialization" (123). Some blogs and social media accounts have been republished as books, not unlike print editions of manuscript diaries. But Cardell observes that many individuals are undertaking rematerialization on their own, including making use of commercial enterprises that repackage digital content as commemorative books in an effort to preserve and cherish what seems transitory and trivial online ("Modern" 505–6). Many diary apps tout users' ability to export, sync, print out, and publish their diary entries as desirable sales points. Users may also be motivated to reclaim their content by downloading, copying, backing up, or printing out because they have lost faith in the trustworthiness of digital platforms.

The movement across paper and digital formats also occurs in the opposite direction, driven in part by nostalgia for old, handwritten diary manuscripts. A number of diarists post pictures of their diary manuscripts on their blogs or via photo-sharing networks like Instagram. Although these texts can be compared to the digitized diaries explored in Chapter 2, the key distinction is that diarists present their own manuscript pages, transforming digitization into an extension of their original diary authorship.

Described as "retro-blogging" (Day 216), this practice makes diarists into archivists of their own past writing, as they seek to preserve and catalog their diaries. Some diarists also use online formats to celebrate the visual artistry or craftsmanship of their diaries, such as in "page through" bullet journal videos. A corollary to these self-digitization practices can be seen in the circulation of manuscript diaries though online formats, including Twitter accounts that reproduce historical diaries by writers like Martha Ballard (@Martha_Ballard), Robert Hooke (@HookesLondon), and Bud Murphy (@TrapperBud). This form of media crossing highlights the parallels between diary entries and tweets as short, segmented, timestamped, and chronologically organized forms of self-documentation. All of these examples point to the important intersections between diary manuscripts and digital diaries, which despite their many differences remain linked in meaningful ways.

- What are the formal, stylistic, or visual parallels between diary manuscripts and digital diaries?
- In what ways do diary manuscripts and digital diaries differ, particularly in terms of their materiality or technological affordances?

Diary Subjects and the Mediated Self

It is conventionally thought that diarists write about themselves and for themselves, thereby articulating an autobiographical sense of self. However, as we saw in the examination of this convention in Chapter 3, scholars generally agree that diarists do not simply represent the self but instead construct a version of the self through the act of writing, a perspective that acknowledges the complex nature of identity and the influence of socio-historical context upon individual subjectivity. Digital diaries enhance these attributes of the diary subject because the self represented online is inherently multiple, shifting, adaptable, and reactive. Digital diaries have been invested with many of the utopian claims made about online culture and digital mediums in general, and that promise individuals democratic access, a platform from which to make a global impact, and the political, social, and economic empowerment that is thought to flow from online engagement. Yet, digital diaries are also acknowledged as reflecting the limitations of these promises, as individual self-expression gets coopted by corporations and manipulated for political gain. Andreas Kitzmann summarizes this tension,

> On the one level the increased control [of the individual over their digital life narrative] could be interpreted as leading to a potential increase in creative and expressive agency. On another level the increased control is actually market driven … firmly codified within the overall matrix of the media-technology-consumer complex.
>
> (*Saved* 45)

The digital diary subject is a mediated self, whose ability to control the documentation of their lives is complicated by the competing demands of the technology they employ, the audiences they interact with, and the commercial and political forces at work upon them.

Despite the differences between analog and digital diaries, many readers approach digital diaries with expectations informed by traditional diary writing, most notably that the digital diarist's self-representation will be truthful. In fact, readers demand full and frank self-disclosure, immediate updates, and timely responses perhaps more emphatically in online environments than in other mediums. Ironically, these expectations are related to the reality that it is supremely easy to misrepresent the self online. Most people present selective versions of themselves in their digital identities but many also use avatars, personas, or pseudonyms, or write anonymously, raising concerns about the accuracy of the subject. Does writing anonymously increase or decrease the likelihood that the self-representation is honest and transparent? Writing about sex workers who blog anonymously, Cardell concludes "anonymity becomes an argument in two directions of belief: secrets are both validated (the author is anonymous because this is so real) and unsettled (the author is anonymous because this is a fake)" (*Dear* 105). As the number of online hoaxes proliferates and readers develop an increased awareness of the possibility that even the most self-revealing blog or social media account could be fake, their focus on the truth of the diary self – and their rage against and punishment of individuals who fail to uphold this expectation – become pronounced features of digital culture.

The ability of digital authors to edit or revise their self-representations also creates anxiety regarding truthfulness in digital diaries. Whereas revisions to diary manuscripts often leave material evidence like crossed out passages or torn pages, revising electronic documents can leave no visible trace (Sorapure 4). Under these circumstances, how can readers trust that diarists have presented an accurate version of themselves? If digital diarists have the means by which to edit their diaries, they also have an incentive to do so in the stringent demands that readers make. "[T]he constant, expectant gaze of prospective audiences creates a rhetorical situation that pressures us to take on … the roles of curator, dramaturge, and censor of our moment-to-moment performances of selfhood within our online networks" (McNeill and Zuern xxvi). While a blogger may know that to retroactively delete or rewrite a blog post will cause their readers to question the blog's authenticity, the competing demand of living up to the standards of their online community can be a powerful motivation. From a literary studies perspective both the original post and the revisions are authorial acts that constitute the diary subject, but the inaccessibility of the electronic record of revision can thwart this approach.

Digital diarists have a host of options in terms of how to document their lives and the variety of platforms and devices appears to substantiate the promise of inclusiveness and diversity within online culture. Yet, many studies of digital media suggest that the selves represented online are strikingly homogenous and skew toward compliance with rather than inversion of social norms, fostering what Mikaela Pitcan et al. call a "vanilla self" (163). These scholars conclude that digital self-representation cultivates a conventional version of the self that minimizes the particularities of identity and replicates hegemonic norms. While many online writers feel the pressure to comply, defying norms presents particular risks for members of marginalized communities. Despite the promise of digital platforms to support and promote alternative identities, rebellious and unconventional voices, and radical social critics, they may instead funnel individuals into safe and predictable molds, resulting in digital diaries that are self-consciously designed to conform to dominant ideologies.

Thus far this discussion of the digital diary subject has focused on intentional acts of self-representation but a great deal of personal digital data is generated without the active agency or explicit consent of individuals. The resulting *involuntary diaries* may still record many details of the individual's daily life but they raise difficult questions regarding the nature of diary writing. As McNeill declares, "We can no longer think of the autobiographical as an individual narrative generated by an autonomous subject" ("There" 66). Instead, corporations increasingly compose "shadow" auto/biographies out of the data they collect about people's online transactions, communication records, and social media activity (77). Of course, the commercialization of personal data is not limited to involuntary records. Every computer-mediated act from an intentionally self-revealing post on Facebook to an online purchase has the potential to be captured and logged. Although comparing these massive, electronic caches of information to diaries may prove useful, doing so requires a substantial reconceptualization of the traditional ways of thinking about the individuality, subjectivity, and agency of the diary subject.

- How does the networked nature of the digital diary subject influence how diarists represent themselves?
- How do digital diarists contend with the questions surrounding truthfulness, authenticity, anonymity, and revision/self-editing in online life writing?
- In what ways do digital diarists comply with or resist the homogenization of digital culture? What are the consequences?
- What do involuntary diaries or data collection technologies indicate about the diary as a record of the self?

Public Privacy and Networked Readers

The public nature of digital diaries is routinely cited as the most significant difference between traditional diaries and digital diaries. While some digital diary platforms provide mechanisms for diarists to limit who has access to their writing, such as diary apps or online programs that tout their password/passcode protection and encryption technologies, many digital diaries are composed on devices or websites that are openly accessible to readers. Some argue that this characteristic automatically disqualifies online or networked writing from being classified as a diary. Bonnie Nardi et al. pose the question, "Would you let 900 million people read your diary?," highlighting the apparent contradiction between a massive online audience and the practice of intimate self-revelation. However, previous discussions of privacy in this book have shown that diary privacy is a complex concept that rarely aligns with a simple public/private binary and that most diaries are written with an awareness of audience. Thus, the fact that many digital diaries have readers does not constitute a fundamental difference from their paper antecedents. Rather, it is the scale of the audience, the immediacy of reader reaction or interaction, the affordances of networked technology, and the commercialization of digital diary content that adapt old features and introduce new ones to the traditional diary.

Perhaps the most surprising aspect of digital diaries is that the potential for 900 million or more readers does not have a greater impact upon their content. The content of analog and digital diaries has more in common than not. Both record the ordinary routines of daily life, reflect on personal struggles, document relationships, and confess intimate experiences. Scholars have developed a number of ways to communicate the seeming contradictory nature of these revelations including "private writing done in public" (Cardell, *Dear* 108); "publically private" and "privately public" (Lange); "public privacy" and "connected privacy" (Kitzmann, *Saved* 80, 91); and "networked privacy" (Marwick and boyd). These phrases strive to make sense of the fact that the public nature of digital media does not eradicate privacy but instead enhances it, making individuals feel comfortable and, at times, compelled to share personal content online. Scholars observe that many digital mediums successfully cultivate a feeling of privacy in users, despite the concrete evidence of publicity. Viviane Serfaty theorizes that the interactive hardware of the screen functions as a veil that makes digital diarists feel invisible. She writes, "Thanks to the screen, diarists feel they can write about their innermost feelings without fearing identification and humiliation, readers feel they can inconspicuously observe others and derive increased understanding and sometimes power from that knowledge" (13). Helen Kennedy has also identified how the intangible experience of "feeling anonymous" – which she distinguishes from actually "being anonymous" – encourages a confessional style of writing online (35). These feelings are so powerful and effective they create a culture of diaristic self-disclosure that cuts across digital platforms and influences many authors/users who would never identity as diarists. It is for this reason that many see the diary expanding rather than shrinking in prominence in the twenty-first century.

However, the prevalence of diary-like confessional writing online also generates anxiety and outrage. Historically, the traditional diary was criticized as a narcissistic genre that encouraged individuals to focus solely on themselves and neglect their commitments to others. Digital diaries are subject to similar criticism, though they are often accused of causing negative consequences on the global rather than individual scale. Characterized as a modern "narcissism epidemic," the twenty-first century culture of self-disclosure is attributed to the prevalence of social media and linked to other pathological behaviors like exhibitionism, bullying, and an inability to empathize with others (Williams). The term "oversharing" is frequently used to describe the phenomenon of posting private, embarrassing, and even shameful content on digital platforms. These critiques emphasize the newness of these social threats, which are seen as magnified by the technological affordances of mass circulation, anonymous interactivity, and the longevity of digital records.

The nature of online or networked diary writing also has significant implications for authorship because authorship is reframed in digital environments as a collaborative act. Readers are understood to play a indispensable role as coproducers of digital content with every "like," repost, link, comment, share, or reply serving as a form of collaboration. The historical diary archive shows that reader interactivity occurred in paper formats as well. Many diaries have readers' comments in their margins and some diaries were collaboratively written (see Chapter 3). Yet, this aspect of the diary is intensified by digital technology, which blurs the distinction between author and reader by making authors reactive to their readers and transforming authors into readers/respondents as well. For the most part, being successful participants in digital culture involves continuous and circular acts of posting and responding. McNeill characterizes the obligation users have to generate and respond to others' online activity as an "exigence" or an urgent need to participate ("Life" 148). Aimée Morrison describes the specific techniques Facebook employs to create this exigence or to "coax" its users to participate in the cocomposition of the website's content; as she notes, "a steady stream of status updates is important to Facebook" (115). Thus, while the networked nature of digital media means that readers can be seen as coauthors, the obligatory nature of reader/author interactivity complicates the concepts of authorial autonomy and authentic self-representation in the diary.

The impact of readers upon digital diaries is also increasingly seen through the lens of risk management. Readers are not just supportive collaborators whose own practices of self-disclosure create healthy online communities defined by shared values. Instead, trolling, doxxing, identity theft, online stalking, catfishing, and a host of other pernicious activities demonstrate that the confessional culture cultivated by many digital platforms exposes authors to real threats. McNeill and Zuern write that "being private in public" creates "a climate of exposure and risk in which identity becomes not only something we are constantly compelled to construct but also something we are constantly compelled to safe-guard against threats to its integrity and security" (viii). Again, these risks are not necessarily new – traditional diaries have often exposed their authors to personal crises, public scandal, or worse – but the immediacy of the danger, the potential for widespread publicity, and the obstacles erected by corporations to prevent individuals from controlling their data privacy create serious challenges for digital diarists.

While many identify the publicity and interactivity of digital diaries as the traits that most distinguish traditional and digital diaries, in my opinion it is the commercialization of diary content that emphatically differentiates the two. Predigital diaries are not immune to commercialization. As addressed in Chapter 2, the process of editing and publishing diaries is directly tied to issues of ownership, copyright, and profit. However, digital media generates profit on an exponentially larger scale and does so by coopting individual user's content, often without their knowledge or consent. Many cultural critics have condemned the ways that social media and other platforms make individual life stories into products to be bought and sold. Today writing a diary with pen and paper can be viewed as a radical act not because it restores the privacy of the past but because it insulates diarists from the modern dangers of predatory corporations and state-sponsored surveillance.

- What aspects of the myth of the private diary are preserved or revised within digital formats?
- Why do people write about private or personal matters on digital platforms or devices? What incentives do they have do to so? What risks do they face?
- How does audience impact why and how individuals write digital diaries?
- How do the prominent critiques of digital diary writing as narcissistic or as commercialized shape diarist's choices in terms of self-representation?

Diary Time Online

Time is a defining feature of the diary genre, evident in the familiar conventions of dated headings, chronological sequence, and diurnal or daily entries. As explained in Chapter 3, these devices root the diary in the middle of experience, representing the events of the day from a present tense perspective. Indeed, the expectation of diary truthfulness is implicitly linked to the immediacy of the written record. Digital diaries preserve these conventions, while taking advantage of technological affordances to speed up their creation and responsiveness. Like their analog counterparts, digital diaries focus on "now," on recording the immediate events of the day with a present tense voice. This impacts what digital diarists write about, when they write, and how their writing gets judged. Digital technology presents writers/users with the ability to respond "in real time," collapsing the gap between an experience and its record. Ruth Page discusses the high value placed on "recency" in digital writing, as timestamps become markers of legitimacy and importance (188). But the pressure to produce a simultaneous documentation of experience increases for many writers/users the feeling of digital exigence, or the compulsive need to stay connected, reactive to events, and up-to-date (McNeill, "Life" 148).

Readers of digital diaries are trained by technological platforms and devices to judge the content of these texts according to their recency. Simultaneity is equated with truthfulness, authenticity, and significance. Hope Wolf writes about Twitter, "the capacity of tweets to narrow the temporal gap between writers' experiences and readers' knowledge of them considerably contributes to their affective power" (1359). For many, the speed at which digital diaries are written and made public stands in pointed contrast to the slow process by which paper diaries are composed and eventually made available to readers through publication or digitization. Wolf notes that the time lag between the composition and publication of analog diaries awakens a fear that the diary has been edited or manipulated, whereas digital diaries use their immediacy to prove they offer unmediated truth (1359). Different digital interfaces allow users different degrees of editorial control including, as mentioned above, the ability to edit their digital texts without leaving any trace. Yet, the temporality of online writing and its perceived closeness to the events described encourage readers to place their faith in the authenticity of timestamped digital texts.

The major difference between time in traditional and digital diaries has to do with how readers encounter or navigate the text. The material nature of bound notebooks or print books influences how readers move through traditional diaries. While readers can skip around and read entries out of order in these formats, they typically follow the one-page-after-the-other structure of the codex. Digital diaries present readers with an entirely different temporal path. Most digital platforms and devices grant readers access to the most recent content first. The reverse chronological order privileges the newest updates or posts, making it easier for readers to consume what appears "in real time" rather than to dig into older material. If readers do choose to read beyond the immediate, they have myriad choices of how to do so: reverse-chronologically, by topic or keyword, by popularity, randomly, following links or search results, and so forth. These reading practices give readers a large degree of autonomy, furthering the argument that they function as cocreators of digital texts by virtue of devising their own order and meaning out of the parts of the text that they access. At the same time, these possibilities make it more likely that the diary will be read as a fragmented or partial text. Soapure notes the high probability that each entry will be "thought of as standing on its own," disembedded from its original context or from its place in a sequence of self-expressions (15). Thus, while digital diary writing generally occurs in chronological order, the texts are read and circulated in ways that fundamentally disrupt the notion of linear time.

- What aspects of diary time are preserved or revised in the digital diary?
- How do digital diaries seek to tap into the value placed on recency or immediacy in digital culture?
- What options do readers have for navigating the digital diary and how do these impact their understanding of the diary's temporal character?

Reading Analog Diaries in the Digital Age

This chapter has proposed that many forms of digital life writing and networked communication benefit from being read through the lens of the traditional, predigital diary. I conclude by suggesting that the opposite is true as well. Digital diaries have lessons to teach us about how to read and interpret traditional diaries. Similar to the relationship between the diary and diary fiction addressed in Chapter 4, it makes sense to think of the digital diary as an outgrowth of the traditional diary because traditional diaries predate their digital counterparts. But in the twenty-first century many people will have far more exposure to digital diaries than traditional ones. Many will learn about the diary and the practices of self-reflection, memory preservation, and so forth from their exposure to digital diaries. Some will turn to analog diaries only after formative experiences using social media or other digital formats, and some will write analog diaries at the same time that they have lively, multi-platform digital lives. The interrelatedness of analog and digital diaries promises to only increase over time.

Moreover, digital diaries should encourage us to reconsider some established myths about traditional diaries. The ease that so many people have with writing about personal and intimate topics in online formats is a strong incentive to recalibrate the claim that truthful confessional writing only happens in private. The role that readers have as collaborative influences upon digital diaries should draw increased attention to diaries that were coauthored or circulated to limited audiences in the past. The fact that online readers can also present threats can teach us to assess the risks and costs associated with autobiographical self-representation, perhaps offering a sobering explanation for why some communities are under-represented in the diary archive. The exciting role that multimedia technology plays in providing digital diarists with audio, visual, photographic, and other modes of expression can point us toward a host of nonnarrative or even nonlanguage-based texts that might not have previously been considered diaries, but which show a similar effort to make use of diverse media to represent the self. Along these lines, if we can legitimately claim Fitbit data, Facebook status updates, diary apps, and GPS records as diaries, we could conceivably claim an equally wide range of predigital, diary-like materials that were formerly excluded from the genre because they did not look enough like handwritten, chronologically organized, personal records of individual lives. Altogether, these lines of analysis demonstrate that the analog diary is not only relevant to an understanding of the popularity, pervasiveness, and influence of digital diaries, but that the diary can be productively reexamined in light of its digital descendants. Indeed, the time may come when we can dispense with the distinguishing terms "analog" and "digital" in favor of the already expansive term "diary."

Essential Question #5: Is the Diary Obsolete, Particularly in the Age of Social Media?

Since the beginning of twenty-first century, numerous essays, articles, and blog posts have been written about the decline of the diary. Many of these works stoke alarmist fears about what the end of diary writing portends about humanity and its future. In 2012, the *New York Times* introduced a "Room for Debate" forum on the diary with the question, "In such a fast-paced, constantly plugged-in society, are we losing the ability to write about our lives in an honest, heartfelt way – or even archive them at all?" ("Will"). For the most part, the blame for the decline in diary writing is laid squarely upon social media, which is characterized as a form of self-representation incompatible with or outright hostile to the old-fashioned diary. Jane Shilling highlights this seeming opposition in an article titled "What Point the Secret Diary in the Instagram Age?" while Connor Hutchingson laments the "lost art of keeping a diary," which he describes as "A hobby that used to be a regular part of daily life for many, [which] now only seems to be an archaic form of expression living on in a minority." In "Will Social Media Kill Writers' Diaries?," Michele Filgate expresses a specific anxiety about the potential consequences if important authors stop writing diaries. She writes,

> It used to be that many writers' diaries were published posthumously ... But what does the age of social media mean for correspondence and diaries? Are tweets and Facebook status updates and Tumblr posts and emails replacing journals and letters? And if so, are we losing something in the process?

Eulogies for the diary like these sometimes address the related phenomenon of handwriting disappearing as a skill and particularly as a subject taught in primary education. Anne Trubek notes that for many "the ability to write by hand is connected to core values" such as intelligence, individuality, and civilization (2). Thus, the inability or unwillingness to write a traditional, handwritten diary gets conflated with the potential downfall of other ideals or institutions: privacy, self-reflection, artistry, autonomy, and society itself.

Yet, for the most part, the idea that diaries are becoming obsolete is tied more to stereotypes associated with the genre than to a reliable record of declining numbers. The rhetoric surrounding the "lost art" of the diary redeploys formative myths of the diary, including the belief that diaries are or should be handwritten manuscripts. The perception that handwritten documents are more intimate, immediate, and trustworthy is a powerful one, and generates nostalgia for paper diaries. This myth remains prominent despite the proliferation of online or digital forms of diary writing, discussed in Chapter 5. In addition, those who lament the decline of the diary are usually motivated by a belief in the beneficial nature of diary writing for individuals and for society as a whole. It is striking that the fear that diaries are falling out of favor generates rhetoric that implicitly rebuts another influential diary myth, namely that diaries are narcissistic. I examine both sides of the debate over whether diaries have positive or negative effects on individuals in Chapter 6. It is worth noting here that the condemnation of social media as a space of oversharing, exhibitionism, and celebrity-seeking confers upon the traditional diary a status as humble, discreet, and respectable that it has not always been granted in the past.

Is there any truth to the idea that less people are writing diaries, particularly given the popularity and accessibility of social media? A 2013 survey rejects this argument, claiming that 83 percent of surveyed British teenage girls keep paper diaries (Gordon). While it is impossible to reliably extrapolate from this survey to make global claims, there is significant evidence that diary writing continues to play a formative role in people's lives. In fact, the diary appears to be growing in appeal to younger writers. The online teen magazine *Rookie* began publishing excerpts from its readers' diaries in 2017, the same year that a query by the magazine to its readers generated a host of enthusiastic responses regarding why diary writing was valuable to them (Miller, "Here"). And, while some remain uneasy with claiming social media and other digital writing as diaries, many have embraced this idea wholeheartedly. As Jess Zimmerman states, "Social media is our modern diary."

Is the diary obsolete? It would be more accurate to say that the diary adapts and endures. While some persist in believing that diaries are objects from the past, associated with quill pens, yellowed paper, and dusty archives, the genre has an ongoing presence in the modern world. Whether diarists are employing pen and paper or keyboards and screens, the diary continues to serve an important role for individuals and for the cultures and societies they inhabit. In fact, as many scholars have noted, the diary should be recognized for its incredible ability to adapt to new cultures, historical periods, and technologies. Kylie Cardell declares that the diary is a "genre of the future" ("Future" 347), a rallying cry for readers to acknowledge that the long history of the genre has produced a form of self-representation that is nimble, expedient, and very often trailblazing.

6 Why Diarists Write

Why do people write diaries? Their motives are as many and diverse as the people themselves, leading to diaries that are also widely varied. Being able to identify and interpret some of the most common reasons people write diaries provides an additional lens through which to analyze them. Examining motives also opens up a conversation about consequences: How does writing a diary shape the diarist's life? Can a diary have an impact beyond the individual diarist? Can diary writing influence the world at large? For the most part, people tend to think of diary writing as having positive motives and effects, such as promoting self-understanding or self-improvement. Diary writing is also often understood to have a positive social impact. For many diarists, keeping a diary is a form of social or political engagement. They see the benefits of diary writing as going far beyond the individual and having the potential to impact the wider world. At the same time, questions are raised about whether diaries might also have negative effects upon individuals or upon communities. Many fear that diary writing promotes narcissism and self-absorption, preventing healthy relationships with others. And some question whether diary writing might actually function as a form of political oppression, surveillance, or self-policing. In other words, while the motives and consequences are often positive for individuals and for communities, there can also be challenges and costs associated with the act of writing a diary.

This chapter explores the question of why diarists write diaries by pursuing two threads of analysis. The first section addresses this topic by applying a cultural and historical framework. This section explores diary writing as a practice that occurs within specific historical moments or cultures and communities. It examines how some diarists understand diary writing to be a collective, public, or political act that supersedes their individual needs or goals. And it explores the potential for diary writing to liberate and empower – or, alternately, to indoctrinate and disenfranchise. The second part of the chapter approaches the question of why diarists write from the perspective of psychology, education, and self-help. This section thinks about the popular conception of the diary as a practice that promotes mental health, productivity, and happiness, and examines academic studies that promote or contest this view. Like the first, this section also balances a discussion of the benefits of the diary against the potential costs or consequences for diarists, including the promotion of narcissism, rumination, or isolation. The two sections of the chapter explore diary writing through research within several distinct scholarly disciplines but arrive at similar conclusions regarding the complex motives that drive diarists and the effects diary writing can have upon individuals and their communities.

History, Politics, and Empowerment

It is conventional to think of diary writing as an individualistic and deeply personal activity, designed primarily to benefit the diarist. Yet many diarists perceive their diaries as having a social or collective function, contributing to a community or to the world as a whole. For these diarists, the genre is a form of political writing. Whether published or not, their diaries provide them with a textual space to respond to, intervene in, or protest the social or political circumstances that define their lives. In this section I explore these motives through three overlapping themes: history, politics, and empowerment. As I show, the diary is particularly valuable as a form of resistance for individuals impacted by political trauma or oppression, or for those who identify with marginalized or vulnerable communities. Yet, as we will also see, not everyone agrees that diaries have positive political effects. Counter-examples of forced diary writing and self-indoctrination prove that diaries can be employed for many, conflicting political reasons.

Some diarists write because they are aware of themselves as historical actors. They recognize that they are living through a significant historical period and view their diaries as having documentary value. By recording the events they are experiencing or witnessing, these diarists self-consciously understand themselves to be participating in the writing of history. Indeed, at moments of great social upheaval, it is common for a call to be issued to the public to take up diary writing for the greater good. For example, in the aftermath of World War I, the Mass Observation project encouraged ordinary English citizens to begin keeping diaries and ultimately collected hundreds of diaries from the 1930s to the 1960s (Moran 145). A similar call was issued to Americans after the election of Donald Trump to the U.S. Presidency in 2016 by Rebecca L. Erbelding, an archivist at the U.S. Holocaust Memorial Museum, who urged historians to keep a daily record in order to help future historians understand this transformative moment (Zamudio-Suaréz). Journalist Summer Brennan issued a more explicitly political call for personal writing as a form of resistance to Trump's politics, which she feared were a prelude to authoritarianism. She exhorted writers to

> [g]et a diary or journal and write down as many words as you can that relate to the things that you value. Fascism favors sameness; it represents a desertification of language and thinking. You can fight sameness with diversity. Inside this thought-desert, we must learn to be jungle oases.
>
> (Brennan)

Of course many diarists do not choose to be historical actors or voluntarily take on the role of public historian. Rather, they are caught up within historical events such as war, genocide, famine, displacement, natural disaster, or other catastrophic experiences.

They may begin writing a diary as these events unfold or, if they were diarists already, they may reorient the function of their diaries to represent these new and traumatic experiences.

Diaries designed to document history require us to reconsider what diaries are for and how they serve their authors. These diarists may choose to write about public events rather than personal experiences or to frame their individual experiences within the historical context. In doing so, they erode the distinction between self and other, employing themselves as a vehicle for documenting what is happening to the community or to the world. Even when writing from the perspective of the "autobiographical I," these diarists speak for others. In addition, diarists who possess a sense of themselves as historians are generally writing to someone. The precariousness of their circumstances introduces the need to address a reader, usually understood as someone in the future or someone who has escaped the diarist's plight. We saw in Chapter 3 that the figure of the reader is influential in many diaries, but the reader can take on particular poignancy in these diaries because they represent the hope that someone will survive to remember those who perish. Yet questions remain about the role diary writing plays for individuals caught up in large-scale and traumatic events: What benefits, if any, does self-writing give to people who are living in the most perilous times? Does it help them survive? Does it provide them with a means of responding, especially if direct action might not be possible? Or is it an inadequate way of reacting to events that demand intervention or resistance?

Diaries written by the victims and survivors of the Holocaust provide insight into these questions. David Patterson describes the motive that caused many people to begin writing diaries during the Holocaust as a "summons," a powerful moral and religious drive to preserve their experiences in writing (30). This idea is echoed by the diarists themselves, including Chaim A. Kaplan (Polish, 1880–1942/43?), whose diary documents the experiences of the Jews trapped in the Warsaw Ghetto. He writes, "a strange idea has stuck in my head since the war broke out – that [writing a diary] is a duty I must perform. This idea is like a flame imprisoned in my bones, burning within me, screaming: Record!" (May 2, 1940). Kaplan's diary exhibits the two characteristics described earlier: It is a record of a people, not a person, and he identifies his diary as written for an audience, albeit an audience that inhabits a future he increasingly understands he will not live to see himself.

> Some of my friends and acquaintances … urge me, in their despair, to stop writing. "Why? For what purpose? Will you live to see it published?["]… And yet, in spite of it all I refuse to listen to them. I feel that continuing this diary to the very end of my physical and spiritual strength is a historical mission which must not be abandoned.
>
> (July 26, 1942)

For Kaplan and other diarists writing during the Holocaust, an overriding motive was to compose a historical record of the Jewish experience, a particularly urgent motive in the face of Nazi efforts to manipulate public perception. Not only did the Nazis disseminate propaganda and misinformation regarding the genocide, they destroyed Jewish archives, libraries, books, and personal records in order to repress counter-narratives. In this context diary writing became a tool for survival, remembrance, and resistance as diarists employed the diary to preserve and restore value to Jewish lives. Ultimately, the imperative to document the Holocaust is inextricable from the imperative to prevent future atrocities, premised upon the belief that knowledge of the truth will provoke readers to act. Can Kaplan and other diarists documenting the Holocaust be said to have succeeded in this goal? As historical records, Holocaust diaries demonstrate the power of the diary to preserve stories that would otherwise have been erased. As testimonials, Holocaust diaries teach readers about the dangers of authoritarianism, race and ethnic bias, and religious intolerance. In pursuing these goals diarists prove that public and political action are compatible with the traditional use of the diary for self-narration.

The political dimension of the diary becomes evident in other historical moments defined by the struggle over public speech, minority representation, and civil rights. During the early decades of the HIV/AIDS crisis (1980s–1990s), many of those impacted by the disease began writing diaries in a deliberate effort to counter the social stigmas projected upon people infected with HIV/AIDS, including the homophobia experienced by the gay men who were the most heavily impacted demographic. In the early years, when little governmental or medical effort was being made to address the spread of the disease, activists understood that it was necessary to tell the stories of those impacted in order to galvanize change. The slogan "Silence = Death" was developed to convey the urgency of recording and circulating their stories. Diary writing was one of the ways in which this slogan was put into practice. In taking up the diary for this political purpose, diarists once again reframed the function of the genre from the individualistic and introspective to the collective and public. Many diarists understood themselves to be representative figures, documenting the plight afflicting those who were silenced by indifference, discrimination, or death. In his diary Eric Michaels (American, 1948–1988) describes diary writing as a practice designed to resist the "process of labeling" that accompanied an HIV/AIDS diagnosis. He affirms the idea that "diary-keeping might serve to keep another set of definitions going," providing him with a space where he could determine how his life and death were depicted (4–5). But Michaels recognizes that the testimonial role of his diary requires a reconsideration of the genre and its relationship to audience:

> For whom do I write? And, worse yet, from what position? I could hedge and claim that I write for myself, in the hope that I can preserve for myself some clarity in a process which is likely to become very clouded very soon … Do I imagine such a text will be read, or even published? Necessarily, a missive (missile) from the grave (which of course solves, or at least hijacks, the question of positioning).
>
> (4)

The use of the diary genre to raise awareness about the experiences of people with HIV/AIDS persists into the present, as the pandemic continues to afflict many vulnerable communities. In 2004 Thembi Ngubane (South African, 1985–2009) began keeping an audio diary of her experiences with HIV/AIDS, which was broadcast by the radio show and podcast *Radio Diaries*. Ngubane's audio diary gave her a public platform through which to address the spread of the disease in South Africa, which has the highest number of people with HIV/AIDS in the world. The primary political intervention of diary representations such as these is to galvanize readers and listeners to take action. Ross Chambers argues that AIDS diaries follow the structure of a relay, handing off the responsibility and urgency of political action to the audience. He writes, "the suspension of a diary on its author's death is perceived to transmit an obligation to continue the work of witness" (7). In fact, according to Chambers, the survival of the diarist "hangs on their successful recruitment of the reader as an appropriate agent of the continued witness their own interrupted testimonial demands" (32). The reader bears the burden of transforming the intimate diary reading experience into a public and political response to the conditions of silence, apathy, or discrimination that contributed to the diarist's illness or death.

The political function of the diary does not only take the form of public protest or collective action. It can also take the form of personal empowerment. Some writers have understood the diary as a form of self-expression that resists destructive social or cultural messages and constitutes a positive self-image. The diary provides a space for articulating a counter-narrative wherein the diarist determines the defining features of their identity, whether or not those meet with approval from the world at large. Black feminist writer and educator bell hooks (American, 1952–) describes how writing a diary as a child was her means of surviving in an environment where she felt her sense of self was under threat. "It was for me the space for critical reflection, where I struggled to understand myself and the world around me, that crazy world of family and community, that painful world" (5). hooks acknowledges that diary writing was available to her as a tool of survival precisely because the genre was perceived as feminine and insignificant. "Confessional writing in diaries was acceptable in our family because it was writing that was never mean to be read by anyone … This was 'safe' writing" (4). But contrary to her family's belief that diary writing would keep hooks compliant to the norms of feminized behavior, she discovers instead that it encouraged her to question gender norms. Through a lifelong practice of diary writing, hooks learned to use the genre for self-transformation and empowerment, what she describes as "writing which offers to us a space where we are able to confront reality in such a way that we live more fully" (11). The language that hooks uses to describe diary writing demonstrates how, for her, the diary is simultaneously personal and political. In crafting a self-narrative in her diary that displayed and valued her intelligence and creativity, hooks also produced a radical response to a society that seeks to keep black women subjugated and disempowered.

Thus far my discussion of the historical and political function of the diary has proceeded from several linked assumptions: That diary writing is a voluntary activity. That diary writing is designed to intervene in and protest against oppressive circumstances. And that diary writing has the power to produce positive or ameliorative results for diarists and the larger world. Yet scholars observe that some diary writing can have contrary motives and effects, complicating this characterization of the political efficacy of the genre. For one, diary writing is not always a voluntary undertaking. While the diarists discussed above did not choose their historical circumstances, they did choose diary writing as their mode of response. But there are other instances in which diary writing becomes what Carolyn Steedman terms "enforced narrative." Steedman argues that although we tend to think of autobiographical writing as voluntary – and, indeed, to believe that the capacity of autobiography to represent and constitute the self derives from its voluntary nature – in fact, a great deal of autobiographical narration is extracted or required (25). Think of your own experiences filling out official forms or applications that require you explain, define, or narrate yourself. How does your self-representation change if the reason you write is not intrinsic motivation but external and official requirement? Is a diary still a diary if the author is obligated to write it? For example, British POWs held captive by the Chinese during the Korean War were distributed diaries and obligated to fill them out as a component of a reeducation campaign. While it might seem easy to distinguish these enforced diaries from "real" diaries, Grace Huxford argues that the distinctions may not be as great as we believe. As Huxford writes, "It is dangerous to presume that any life story is the unadulterated and voluntary articulation of selfhood, as all narratives are produced, to some extent, in response to others' demands and in terms others can access" (8). Examples like these disrupt many preconceptions about diaries and show how the diary can be used to subjugate and survey, instead of liberate and empower.

Even outside of the coercive space of a prison, the diary can serve the purpose of controlling and shaping the diarist's behavior in compliance with oppressive social structures. In his study of diaries written by Russians during Stalin's regime, Jochen Hellbeck rejects the expectation that diaries provide individuals living under authoritarian rule with a place to voice resistance. Instead, Hellbeck argues, diaries became a means by which the ideology of the state was internalized, as Russian diarists employed their diaries to self-police and to self-indoctrinate. "Many Soviet diaries were distinctly introspective, but introspection was not linked to individualist purposes … these Soviet diarists revealed an urge to write themselves into their social and political order" (4). The scenario Hellbeck describes has parallels with Michel Foucault's concept of the panopticon, in which the tools of surveillance are internalized. The diary could be what Foucault terms "the panopticisms of every day," a small but powerful mechanism for guaranteeing that individuals shape their thinking and behavior to the rules of their societies, even if those rules ultimately strip them of freedoms (*Discipline* 223). The Soviet diarists wrote voluntarily, but their writing defies the idea that self-expression is an inherently liberating act.

Furthermore, it is worth interrogating the limits of the diary as a form of historical or political writing. Can the diary really intervene in world-changing political or military struggles? Do diarists faced with horrific violence or oppression have reason to believe that their self-writing can make a difference? Alexandra Garbarini identifies a turning point in many Holocaust diaries in the late years of World War II, after which many diarists ceased to believe that writing a diary was a meaningful act of political protest. She states, "Genocide transformed the function of diary writing" (130). While initially the diary gave Jewish writers a way of preserving their culture and protesting their treatment, over time the diary became instead "embedded in their horror-filled circumstances" (137). Writing a diary was psychologically difficult, physically exhausting, and dangerous – no longer a mode of escape or a tool of resistance. While based on the specific conditions of diary writing in the final years of the Holocaust, Garbarini's conclusions prompt a reconsideration of the political power of the diary. Without undercutting the importance of diaries written by individuals during perilous historical moments, it is necessary to consider what diaries can and cannot do to represent and act upon trauma or oppression.

Readers tend to think of diaries as primarily serving their authors as a means of writing the self, preserving memory, or expressing thoughts or emotions that have no other outlet. Yet many diarists conceive of their diaries as fulfilling different goals by serving larger communities, including communities under threat or facing social stigma. They view the diary as a vehicle for constructing a historical narrative that will instruct a future audience about the past, or as an intervention in political events or social structures that threaten inequality or worse. Diaries written with these motives in mind sometimes take forms that differ from the conventional diary: less personal, more historical or documentary, outwardly focused instead of introspective, clearly anticipating and addressing a reader, and seeking to effect a change in the world. However, as I have shown, these goals do not necessarily result in diaries that are progressive or liberating. Diaries can also become forms of furthering social oppression, stripping away individual rights, and enhancing traumatic experience. Readers attentive to the reasons diarists write benefit from exploring these different dimensions of the genre and how they relate to the specific historical and cultural contexts of individual texts.

Self, Health, and Happiness

It is common to think of diary writing as a practice that changes the diarist. Usually the change is understood as an individual phenomenon, in contrast to the social or political interventions discussed above. And, for the most part, the change is characterized as a positive one. The diary is celebrated for its ability to facilitate personal growth, maturation, self-understanding, self-improvement, and an optimistic outlook on life. This view finds support across many fields, including psychology, behavioral science, and education, and pervades many works of popular self-help, including publications devoted to self-care, productivity, and happiness. Yet scholars and writers in these fields also caution that the transformative potential of diary writing is not always supported by research, noting that some studies suggest that, for certain individuals, a diary may provoke or reinforce damaging self-talk or destructive thinking. In this section, I explore these divergent viewpoints through the themes of self, health, and happiness. I introduce studies that advocate for diary writing as a tool for mental health and educational success, while also addressing the studies that counter these claims and that issue warnings about the potential dangers of the diary. This discussion draws upon diarists' own reflections on what diary writing does for them as individuals, including both endorsements of the positive role that the diary plays in their lives and apprehensive fears about how the diary might exacerbate rather than solve their problems.

As we have seen, one of the core claims of autobiography studies is that acts of self-narration like diary writing constitute rather than simply represent the self. It proceeds from this view that narrating the self also has the potential to shape the material, lived experience of the author, impacting not only how they perceive themselves but how they act, respond, or exist in the world. John Paul Eakin describes this as "living autobiographically" and argues that "autobiography is not merely something we read in a book; rather, as a discourse of identity, delivered bit by bit in the stories we tell about ourselves day in and day out, autobiography structures our living" (*Living* 4). As one form of daily autobiographical writing, the diary can be understood to fulfill this role of constructing the self and, in so doing, changing the individual's life or identity. Philippe Lejeune states that "Keeping a journal is first and foremost a way of life"; indeed, he proposes, "Diarists start writing in their diaries throughout the day, while living" (*On Diary* 31, 224). According to these perspectives, it is virtually impossible to separate the narration of the self from the daily acts and experiences of the self, as the conventions of diary writing impact and structure the life that they record. This is a concept supported by many diarists. Susan Sontag (American, 1933–2004) declared, "I create myself. The journal is a vehicle for my sense of selfhood" (December 31, 1957). Later she sums up this idea as, "I write ... in order to find out what I think" (January 3, 1966). In Sontag's eyes the diary is not merely a record or a mirror of the self but a mechanism for creating it.

Studies within the fields of theoretical and clinical psychology extend the perception of diary writing as a form of self-construction by proposing that diaries and other forms of self-narration also have the capacity to improve individual lives. The subfield of narrative psychology builds upon the research of scholars like Bertram J. Cohler, Dan McAdams, and James Pennebaker in order to propose that the stories we tell about ourselves have the potential to alter our self-conception. Psychologists apply these ideas within therapeutic contexts by having patients write self-narratives, a practice known as scriptotherapy. Joanne Frattaroli's analysis of 146 studies on the psychological benefits of self-disclosure demonstrates that there is overwhelming evidence that practices like scriptotherapy are powerful tools for achieving healing in the aftermath of trauma. Writing specifically about the diary, Wendy J. Wiener and George C. Rosenwald identify five main functions that diaries play in diarists' lives: setting boundaries, managing emotions, dissolving boundaries, mirroring the self, and managing time. They conclude that insofar as a healthy sense of self depends upon reflecting on and learning from one's experiences, the diary is the "most serviceable model" for achieving this goal (56). Christina M. Karns et al. further emphasize these findings in their research demonstrating that gratitude journaling alters the brain, producing a demonstrable change in neural activity that can be observed through MRI imaging scans.

These academic arguments have influenced many works of popular psychology including self-help publications that provide guidelines for increasing productivity, mindfulness, and happiness. Diary writing is regularly identified as one of the most practical and influential activities individuals can undertake to improve their lives. For example, in *The Happiness Advantage*, Shawn Achor advocates for what he calls the "positive tetris effect" or the practice of training the mind to focus on the positive by keeping a daily written record of the good things in one's life (100–1). Bill Burnett and Dave Evans' "Designing Your Life" system also relies upon diary writing as a tool for helping individuals develop a clear understanding of what they want out of life. They advocate a practice called the "Good Time Journal," which tracks "peak experiences" in order to zero in on the sources of happiness and fulfillment (58). The use of the diary for recording the highlights of life, rather than simply everyday experiences, has been popularized through gratitude journaling, and numerous self-help books are designed to encourage this practice. Despite their different packaging, each of these approaches promotes the idea that daily writing is a tool for self-reflection and positive thinking that has the potential to enable individuals to remake themselves and their circumstances.

The capacity of diary writing to have positive psychological effects is echoed by studies within the field of education that address the role that the diary can have in improving student performance and outcomes. Diary writing assignments take many forms but can generally be classified as either reflective writing about the class or a student's learning process, directly tied to the class content, or reflective writing about the student's life, in which the student-diarist is not obligated to address the class or their educational experiences. Teachers across a wide spectrum of academic disciplines and educational levels implement diary writing within their classrooms and many studies support the practice as a valuable form of pedagogy (Figure 6.1). Diary

ENGL 4333: Life Writing
University of Texas Arlington

Write Your Life

This assignment asks you to engage in a new form of life writing during the course of the semester. As you study life writing, you will engage in a life writing practice of your own.

Your life writing can take any form but I do ask that you either take up an entirely new kind of life writing or make a significant alteration to an existing life writing practice. For example, you might decide to keep a daily diary during the semester. Or, if you already keep a diary, you might decide to start a blog. Or, if you have blogged occasionally, you might commit to posting weekly. You get the idea. We will discuss other options in class and I encourage students to be creative. But, it must be a *continuous practice* (daily, weekly, bi-weekly, etc.) that you will commit to for the duration of the semester.

Please note: You will not be graded on the quality or content of your life writing, but on your reflection on the practice. You are not be obligated to submit your life writing itself although, depending on your level of comfort, you may choose do so.

Part 1: Write Your Life

1. What kinds of life writing (if any) have you engaged in before this semester? Describe your experiences. What did it mean to you? Why did you begin or end?
2. What new life writing will you engage in this semester? Be specific about what materials or technological medium you will be using. Why did you pick this format?
3. What are your goals? What do you hope to get out ofthe experience? How will you measure the outcome? In other words, how will you and I know whether or not you have been successful?

Part 2: Mid-semester Reflection

1. How is it going? Have you been able to stick to your goals? What unexpected experiences have you had? What obstacles have you encountered?
2. How has the format/medium you selected shaped the content of your life writing? What does the form encourage or discourage in terms of your self narration?
3. How has the reading we have done thus far this semester influenced your life writing? Explore the intersections between the assigned texts/topics and your personal writing. You should make reference to relevant texts from the assigned reading.

Part 3: End-of-semester Reflection

1. How did it go? Did you reach your goals? Were you successful in overcoming obstacles? What strategies did you find most useful?
2. How did your life writing practice shape your interpretation of the literary texts we are reading? What insights did you gain that might not otherwise have been readily apparent?
3. Select one specific entry, aspect, or technique from your life writing and analyze it using the terms and concepts you've learned this semester. To what extent does literary analysis enable you to better understand your own process? You have the option of illustrating this discussion with an example from your life writing (via screenshot, link, photograph, etc.), if you feel comfortable doing so.
4. Will you continue your new life writing practice after the class ends? Why or why not?

Figure 6.1 Sample Educational Diary Assignment: "Write Your Life" writing has been shown to provide numerous benefits for students, including the promotion of critical thinking, active learning, and general psychological well-being. In *Learning Journals*, Jennifer Moon argues that assigned diary writing enhances the conditions that are most favorable to the learning process, including giving students a sense of ownership over their educations and encouraging metacognition or the understanding of their own learning style (26). These benefits have been documented in educational environments ranging from primary schools, where positive thinking journals resulted in an increase in students' well-being that correlated with their capacity to learn (Carter et al.), to college-level literature courses, where the practice of writing learning logs made students into more active participants in the course content (Babcock).

However, scholars of psychology and education do not uniformly affirm the benefits of diary writing. Some psychologists caution against the idea that the diary is an appropriate tool for every individual, asserting instead that diarists require guidance regarding how to utilize the genre and that some should be warned away from the practice altogether. Omer Faruk Simsek observes that self-reflection can lead to self-absorption, particularly if individuals become fixated on arriving at an absolute truth about themselves (1119). These conclusions are reinforced by Daniel Stein and Anthony M. Grant, who warn about the dangers of self-rumination, which they describe as a dysfunctional version of self-reflection that involves dwelling upon the negative aspects of oneself (507). Studies such as these suggest that the self-reflective function of diary writing will not work for everyone and may exacerbate some mental health struggles. Similar cautions can be found in the field of education. Timothy O'Connell and Janet Dyment's analysis of seventy-five publications on reflective journaling in educational environments concludes that despite the fact that most teachers believe diaries can assist their students, the implementation of diary writing in the classroom faces many challenges. They identify eleven major obstacles that interfere with the effectiveness of educational diaries including the fact that most students perceive them as irrelevant busy work and that some assignments reaffirm the gender stereotype of the feminized diary (52). The fact that educational diaries are assigned rather than self-motivated also echoes the concerns that surround the enforced diaries discussed in the previous section. Can students express themselves openly and honestly if they know their diaries will be read and evaluated by their teachers?

Similar hesitations regarding the efficacy of diary writing can be found within many diaries, as diarists confront the potentially unhealthy or self-damaging aspects of their writing practices. Some diarists fear that the diary reinforces obsessive tendencies, giving rise to graphomania, an urgent and unending need to record one's experiences. Sarah Manguso describes her graphomania this way: "Imagining a life without the diary, even one week without it, spurred a panic that I might as well be dead" (3). Other diarists worry that the diary isolates them from friends and family. W. N. P. Barbellion wondered, "Can an engaged or married man conscientiously continue to write his *journal intime*?" (August 6, 1915). For Barbellion, the introspective function of his diary created a sense that the diary threatened his commitment to his future wife. Diarists also worry that keeping a diary will make them either too passive and self-reflective, or too active in pursuit of diary material. Henri-Frédéric Amiel (Swiss, 1821–1881) blamed his diary for his inability to act without inhibition, writing, "[my] timidity springs from the excessive development of the reflective power which has almost destroyed in my all spontaneity, impulse, and instinct, and therefore all boldness and confidence" (July 22, 1855). By contrast, James Boswell describes a friend's concern that "my journal did me harm, as it made me hunt about for adventures to adorn it with" (May 25, 1763). Although Boswell defends his diary from this accusation, elsewhere in his diary he congratulates himself for having dramatic and interesting experiences to record. Perhaps the most damning counter-argument against the diary's beneficial or self-improving qualities relates to the number of prominent diarists who have committed suicide, including Arthur Inman, Sylvia Plath, Cesare Pavese, and Virginia Woolf. As the work of suicidologist David Lester indicates, diaries may provide insight into the reasons individuals commit suicide without offering an explanation for why diary writing failed to fulfill its promise as a form of affirmative self-expression.

Are diaries good for diarists? Do they promote mental health, assist with self-improvement or learning, and contribute to happiness or well-being? Or do diaries promote self-destructive rumination, reinforce obsessive or narcissistic behaviors, and cut diarists off from the reality of their own experiences? The reality is likely somewhere in the middle. Diarists are driven by a variety of motives and experience a variety of effects. Their writing changes over time to meet different needs, respond to different historical or personal circumstances, or adapt to changing popular conceptions of the diary. This section equips readers with the critical contexts to navigate the binary views of diary writing as purely self-affirming or self-destructive and to develop a nuanced conception of the different ways in which diaries may impact the lives of their authors.

Questions to consider:

- Why does the diarist write? What motivates them?
- How do their motives shape what or how they write?
- Does the diary have a positive, negative, or mixed individual or social impact? If so, what is the nature of that impact? How can it be seen or measured?
- What do the motives and impacts of diaries teach us about how diaries function in specific historical or cultural contexts?
- What can diarists do to pursue the positive outcomes of diary writing and to avoid the negative ones?

Conclusion: How to Write a Diary

This book introduces new frameworks for the critical consideration of diaries, pushing back against some of the most familiar and influential myths about the genre. It explores a wide variety of diary forms and conventions, and addresses the paradoxes, ongoing debates, and essential questions surrounding the genre. It references diaries written across the globe, across the long history of the genre, and in diverse mediums ranging from paper manuscripts to microblogging networks. From this book, readers should comprehend that diaries take many forms, accomplish many different goals, and respond to the most recognizable conventions of the genre in unique, creative, and evolving ways.

In the preface to this book, I confessed that while the book is designed to promote the reading, analysis, and appreciation of diaries, a secondary goal is to encourage diary readers to become diary writers. Some readers of this book will already be diarists, or may have once kept a diary. Some will have never considered diary writing at all. I hope that every reader will be inspired by the diary stories in this book to begin a diary or to recommit to their diary writing practice. What follows are a few suggestions about how to do so, directed primarily at those who are not sure where to start.

Where should you start? Based on the diary conventions presented in this book, you might begin by thinking about four things:

Content

What do you want to write about? Do you want to record the basic facts of your day-to-day life? Do you want to explore big ideas or to reflect on your experiences? Should the diary be about a particular topic or theme, indicating your interests or where you want to focus your attention? Do you intend your diary to have a particular function, such as political commentary or self-improvement?

Structure

How will you organize your diary? Will you follow the conventional chronological structure, complete with dated headings? If not, what structure works best for you? How often do you plan to write? How will the structures or rhythms of the diary relate to your planned content?

Audience

Who is your intended audience? If you plan to write only for yourself, what strategies will you employ to guarantee the diary's privacy? If you plan for an audience – or if you simply anticipate that an audience is possible, now or in the future – how will this impact what you write about or how you write?

Medium

What is your planned medium? In other words, what format, tools, materials, or devices you will use to compose your diary? This book has proposed that a diary's medium has a demonstrable impact upon its content. How will your chosen medium shape what you write about or how you write? What will the medium allow you do or in what ways might it limit what is possible?

These general, framing questions should provoke ideas regarding how to begin a diary, but for readers who still feel unsure about where to start, the following diary forms might also prove beneficial.

Gratitude Journal: Write a daily record of positive experiences or things you are grateful for in order to foster a positive outlook on life.

Letter Diary: Address your diary to someone who is important to you. Whether or not you ever share your diary with the addressee, the possibility of speaking to an audience can be very generative.

List Diary: Keep lists of reading, quotes, fragmented thoughts or questions, brief descriptive passages, goals, experiences, and so forth. Because list diaries have no rules and require no cohesion, diarists are free to explore their interests widely.

Key Phrase Diary: Choose a short, thought-provoking phrase to start each diary entry. For example, in *The Folded Clock*, Heidi Julavits begins every diary entry with the phrase "Today I." Others to consider: "Nobody else knows"; "If I could"; "I can't stop thinking about"; "Right now I".

These ideas do not come close to exhausting all the possible ways you might compose your diary. I hope you will be inspired to find your own path, aware that by becoming a diarist you enter into a long and significant literary tradition. This book invited you to fall in love with the experience of reading diaries, but I end here with an invitation to fall in love with the act of diary writing itself.

Bibliography

Primary Works: Diaries and Diary Fiction

al-Radi, Nuha. *Baghdad Diaries: A Woman's Chronicle of War and Exile.* Vintage, 1998.

Alexander, Jeb [Carter Newman Bealer]. *Jeb and Dash: A Diary of Gay Life, 1918–1945.* Edited by Ina Russell. Faber & Faber, 1993.

Alexie, Sherman. *The Absolutely True Diary of a Part-Time Indian.* Little, Brown, 2007.

Alvarez, Julia. *Before We Were Free.* Knopf, 2002.

Amiel, Henri-Frédéric. *Amiel's Journal: The Journal Intime of Henri-Frédéric Amiel.* Translated by Mrs. Humphry Ward. 2 vols. Macmillian, 1894.

Barbellion, W. N. P. [Bruce Frederick Cummings]. *Journal of a Disappointed Man.* Penguin Books, 2017.

Barroux. *Line of Fire: Diary of an Unknown Soldier.* Translated by Sarah Ardizzone. Phoenix Yard Books, 2014.

Bashkirtseff, Marie. *I Am the Most Interesting Book of All: The Diary of Marie Bashkirtseff.* Translated by Phyllis Howard Kernberger and Katherine Kernberger. 2 vols. Chronicle Books, 1997.

Basquiat, Jean-Michel. *The Notebooks.* Princeton UP, 2015.

Bechdel, Alison. *Fun Home: A Family Tragicomic.* Houghton Mifflin, 2006.

Bell, Gabrielle. *Truth is Fragmentary: Travelogues & Diaries.* Uncivilized Books, 2014.

Benedetti, Mario. *The Truce: The Diary of Martín Santomé.* 1960. Translated by Harry Morales. Penguin Books, 2015.

Beti, Mongo. *The Poor Christ of Bomba.* 1956. Translated by Gerald Moore. Waveland Press, 2005.

Bobak, Molly Lamb. *Double Duty: Sketches and Diaries of Molly Lamb Bobak, Canadian War Artist.* Edited by Carolyn Gossage. Dundurn Group, 1992.

Boswell, James. *London Journal, 1762–1763*. Edited by Gordon Turnbell. Penguin, 2013.

Brontë, Anne. *The Tenant of Wildfell Hall*. 1848. Penguin Classics, 1996.

Browning, Elizabeth Barrett. *The Barretts at Hope End: The Early Diary of Elizabeth Barrett Browning*. Edited by Elizabeth Berridge. John Murray, 1974.

Burnett Archive of Working Class Autobiographies, Brunel U. http://bura.brunel.ac.uk/handle/2438/7356

Byatt, A. S. *Possession*. Vintage, 1990.

Cabot, Meg. *The Princess Diaries*. HarperTeen, 2000.

Cate, Eliza Jane. "Susy L—'s Diary," *Holden's Dollar Magazine*, October 1849–March 1850. American Periodicals Online.

Chbosky, Stephen. *The Perks of Being a Wallflower*. Gallery Books, 1999.

Cobain, Kurt. *Journals*. Riverhead Books, 2002.

Coetzee, J. M. *Diary of a Bad Year*. Viking, 2007.

Collins, Wilkie. *The Moonstone*. 1868. Penguin Classics, 1999.

Cortázar. Julio. "The Distances: The Diary of Alina Reyes." 1951. *Blow-Up and Other Stories*. Translated by Paul Blackburn. Pantheon Books, 1963, pp. 17–27.

Couto, Mia. *Sleepwalking Land*. 1992. Translated by David Brookshaw. Serpent's Tail, 2006.

Dang, Thuy Tram. *Last Night I Dreamed of Peace: The Diary of Dang Thuy Tram*. Translated by Andrew X. Pham. Three Rivers Press, 2007.

Davis, Emilie. *Memorable Days: The Emilie Davis Diaries*. Project Director, Judith Giesberg. Villanova U. http://davisdiaries.villanova.edu/

de Beauvoir, Simone. *The Woman Destroyed*. 1967. Translated by Patrick O'Brian. G.P. Putnam's Sons, 1969.

de Guérin, Eugénie. *Journal of Eugénie de Guérin*. Edited by G. S. Trebutien. Simpkin, Marshall, 1865. HathiTrust https://hdl.handle.net/2027/hvd.hwlc6w

de Jesus, Carolina Maria. *The Unedited Diaries of Carolina Maria de Jesus*. Edited by Robert M. Levine and José Carlos Sebe Bom Meihy, translated by Nancy P. S. Naro and Cristina Mehrtens. Rutgers UP, 1999.

Defoe, Daniel. *Robinson Crusoe*. 1712. Edited by Michael Shinagel. 2nd edition. W.W. Norton, 1994.

Ding, Ling. "Miss Sophia's Diary." 1927. *I Myself am a Woman: Selected Writings of Ding Ling*. Edited and translated by Tani E. Barlow. Beacon Press, 1989, pp. 49–81.

Dostoevsky, Fyodor. *Notes from the Underground*. 1864. Translated by Richard Pevear and Larissa Volokhonsky. Vintage Classics, 1994.

Drinker, Elizabeth Sandwith. *The Diary of Elizabeth Drinker.* Edited by Elaine Forman Crane. 3 vols. Northeastern UP, 1991.

Duncan-Wallace, Alexander Munro. *Diary of a Civilian Internee in Singapore 1942–1945.* Royal Commonwealth Society Library, RCMS 103/12/17. U of Cambridge Digital Library. http://cudl.lib.cam.ac.uk/view/MS-RCMS-00103-00012-00017/1

Emerson, Mary Moody. *The Almanacks of Mary Moody Emerson: A Scholarly Digital Edition.* Edited by Noelle A. Baker and Sandra Harbert Petrulionis. https://marymoodyemerson.net/

Emerson, Ralph Waldo. *The Journals and Miscellaneous Notebooks.* Edited by William H. Gilman, George P. Clark, Alfred R. Ferguson, and Merrell R. Davis. 16 vols. Belknap Press of Harvard UP, 1960–1982.

Everett, Percival. *Erasure.* Hyperion, 2001.

Feris, Emil. *My Favorite Thing is Monsters.* Fantagraphic Books, 2016.

Field, Michael [Katharine Bradley and Edith Cooper]. The Online Diaries of "Michael Field." Edited by Marion Thain. *Victorian Lives and Letters Consortium* (Center for Digital Humanities, U South Carolina). http://tundra.csd.sc.edu/vllc/field

Fielding, Helen. *Bridget Jones's Diary.* Viking, 1996.

Filipović, Zlata. *Zlata's Diary: A Child's Life in Sarajevo.* Translated by Christina Pribichevich-Zorić. Viking, 1994.

Flynn, Gillian. *Gone Girl.* Broadway Books, 2012.

Fowles, John. *The Collector.* Vintage, 1963.

Frank, Anne. *The Diary of Anne Frank: The Revised Critical Edition.* Doubleday, 2003.

———. *Anne Frank's Diary: The Graphic Adaptation.* Adapted by Ari Folman, illustrated by David Polonsky. Pantheon, 2018.

Fujii, Takuichi. *The Hope of Another Spring: Takuichi Fujii, Artist and Wartime Witness.* Introduced by Barbara Johns. U Washington P, 2017.

Gide, André. *The Counterfeiters; With "Journal of the Counterfeiters."* 1926. Translated by Dorothy Bussy and Justin O'Brien. Vintage, 1973.

———. *The Notebooks of André Walter.* 1891. Philosophical Library, 2007.

Gillespie, Emily Hawley. *"A Secret to be Buried": The Diary and Life of Emily Hawley Gillespie, 1858–1888.* Edited by Judy Nolte Lensink. U Iowa P, 1989.

Gloeckner, Phoebe. *The Diary of a Teenage Girl.* North Atlantic Books, 2002.

Gobetti, Ada. *Partisan Diary: A Woman's Life in the Italian Resistance.* Edited and translated by Jomarie Alano. Oxford UP, 2014.

Goethe, Johann Wolfgang von. *The Sorrows of Young Werther*. 1774. Translated by Michael Hulse. Penguin, 1989.

Gogol, Nikolay. *Diary of a Madman, The Government Inspector, and Selected Stories*. Translated by Ronald Wilks. Penguin, 2005.

Gombrowicz, Witold. *Diary*. Translated by Lillian Vallee. Yale UP, 2012.

Grimké, Charlotte Forten. *The Journals of Charlotte Forten Grimké*. Edited by Brenda Stevenson. Oxford UP, 1988.

Guerra, Wendy. *Everyone Leaves*. Translated by Achy Obejas. Amazon Crossing, 2006.

Guevara, Ernesto. *The Complete Bolivian Diaries of Ché Guevara*. Edited by Daniel James. Cooper Square Press, 2000.

Guibert, Hervé. *To the Friend Who Did Not Save My Life*. 1990. Translated by Linda Cloverdale. High Risk Books/Serpent's Tail, 1994.

Guo, Xiaolu. *A Concise Chinese-English Dictionary for Lovers*. Anchor Books, 2007.

Harbin, Dustin. *Diary Comics*. 2012–2018. http://dharbin.com/comics/

Highsmith, Patricia. *Edith's Diary*. Simon and Schuster, 1977.

Hillesum, Etty. *Etty Hillesum: An Interrupted Life*. Translated by Arnold J. Pomerans. Henry Holt, 1996.

Hiranandani, Veera. *The Night Diary*. Dial Books, 2018.

Hoby, Margaret. *The Private Life of an Elizabethan Lady: The Diary of Lady Margaret Hoby, 1599–1605*. Edited by Joanna Moody. Sutton, 1998.

Hooke, Robert. *Diary, 1671/2-1683*. London Metropolitan Archives, CLC/495/MS01758. https://search.lma.gov.uk/scripts/mwimain.dll/144/LMA_OPAC/web_

Hustvedt, Siri. *The Blazing World*. Simon and Schuster, 2014.

Inman, Arthur. *The Inman Diary: A Public and Private Confession*. Edited by Daniel Aaron. 2 vols. Harvard UP, 1985.

Japanese American Relocation Digital Archive, U of California. https://calisphere.org/exhibitions/t11/jarda/

Julavits, Heidi. *The Folded Clock: A Diary*. Doubleday, 2015.

Kahlo, Frida. *The Diary of Frida Kahlo: An Intimate Self Portrait*. Translated by Barbara Crow de Toledo and Ricardo Pohlenz. Bloomsbury, 1995.

Kaplan, Chaim A. *Scroll of Agony: The Warsaw Diary of Chaim A. Kaplan*. Translated and edited by Abraham I. Katsh. Macmillian, 1965.

Kashyap, Keshni. *Tina's Mouth: An Existential Comic Diary*. Houghton Mifflin Harcourt, 2012.

Kierkegaard, Søren. *Either/Or*. 1843. Edited by Victor Eremita, translated by Alastair Hannay. Penguin Classics, 1992.

Kinney, Jeff. *Diary of a Wimpy Kid: A Novel in Cartoons*. Amulet Books, 2007.

Kochalka, James. *American Elf*. Vol 1: *The Collected Sketchbook Diaries of James Kochalka*. Top Shelf Productions, 2004.

Kourouma, Ahmadou. *Allah Is Not Obliged*. 2000. Translated by Frank Wynne. Anchor Books, 2007.

Laub, Michel. *Diary of the Fall*. 2011. Translated by Margaret Jull Costa. Other Press, 2014.

Lejeune, Philippe and Catherine Bogaert. *Un Journal à Soi: Histoire d'une Pratique*. Textuel, 2003.

Lermontov, Mikhail. *A Hero of Our Time*. 1840. Translated by Natasha Randall. Penguin Books, 2009.

Lessing, Doris. *The Diary of a Good Neighbor*. 1983. Reprinted in *The Diaries of Jane Somers*. Vintage, 1984.

———. *The Golden Notebook*. 1962. Harper Perennial, 2007.

Lister, Anne. *The Secret Diaries of Miss Anne Lister*. Edited by Helena Whitbread. Virago, 2010.

Livingstone, David. *Livingstone's 1871 Field Diary: A Multispectral Critical Edition*. Project Director, Adrian S. Wisnicki. U of California, Los Angeles. 2011–13. http://livingstone.library.ucla.edu/1871diary/index.htm

Loos, Anita. *Gentlemen Prefer Blondes: The Illuminating Diary of a Professional Lady*. Grosset & Dunlap, 1925.

Lu, Xun. *Diary of a Madman and Other Stories*. Translated by William A. Lyell. U Hawaii P, 1990.

Manguso, Sarah. *Ongoingness: The End of a Diary*. Greywolf Press, 2015.

Maroh, Julie. *Blue Is the Warmest Color*. 2010. Translated by Ivanka Hahnenberger. Arsenal Pulp Press, 2013.

Merrill, James. *The (Diblos) Notebook*. Atheneum, 1965.

Michaels, Eric. *Unbecoming*. Edited by Paul Foss. Duke UP, 1997.

Michitsuna no Haha. *Kagerō Diary*. Edited and translated by Sonja Arntzen. U Michigan P, 1997.

Mills, Claudia. *The Totally Made-Up Civil War Diary of Amanda MacLeish*. Farrar, Straus and Giroux, 2008.

Mitchell, David. *Cloud Atlas*. Random House, 2004.

Moen, Erika. *DAR! A Super Girly Top Secret Comic Diary*. 2003–2009. www.darcomic.com

Murdoch, Iris. *The Sea, The Sea*. 1978. Vintage, 1999.

Nabokov, Vladimir. *Lolita*. Vintage, 1955.

Ngubane, Thembi. *Thembi's AIDS Diary: A Year in the Life of a South African Teenager. Radio Diaries*. www.aidsdiary.org/index.html

Nin, Anaïs. *The Early Diary of Anaïs Nin.* Vol. 1. Translated by Jean L. Sherman. 4 vols. Harcourt Brace Jovanovich, 1978–1985.

Nini, Rachid. *Diario de un ilegal.* 1999. Translated by Gonzalo Fernández Parrilla and Malika Embarek López. Ediciones del oriente y del mediterráneo, 2002.

Nolen, Jerdine. *Eliza's Freedom Road: An Underground Railroad Diary.* Simon and Schuster, 2011.

O'Connor, George and Harmen Van den Bogaert. *Journey into Mohawk Country.* Translated by William Starna and Charles Gehring. First Second, 2006.

Operation War Diary. www.operationwardiary.org/

Orwell, George. *Nineteen Eighty-Four.* Harcourt, Brace, & World, 1949.

Oyeyemi, Helen. "if a book is locked there's probably a good reason for that don't you think?" *What Is Not Yours Is Not Yours: Stories.* Riverhead Books, 2016, pp. 307–25.

Oyono, Ferdinand. *Houseboy.* 1960. Translated by John Reed. Heinemann Educational Books, 1966.

Ozeki, Ruth. *A Tale for the Time Being.* Canongate, 2013.

Palahniuk, Chuck. *Diary.* Anchor Books, 2003.

Parra, Teresa de la. *Iphigenia (The diary of a young lady who wrote because she was bored).* Introduced by Naomi Lindstrom, translated by Bertie Acker. U Texas P, 1993.

Patchen, Kenneth. *The Journal of Albion Moonlight.* Padell, 1941.

Pavese, Cesare. *This Business of Living: Diaries 1935–1950.* Transaction Publishers, 2009.

Pepys, Samuel. *The Diary of Samuel Pepys, 1660–1669.* Edited by Robert Latham and William Matthews. 9 vols. U California P, 1970–1983.

Piglia, Ricardo. *The Diaries of Emilio Renzi: Formative Years.* Translated by Robert Croll. Restless Books, 2017.

Podlubny, Stepan Filippovich. Diary (excerpts). *Intimacy and Terror: Soviet Diaries of the 1930s.* Edited by Véronique Garros, Natalia Korenevskaya, and Thomas Lahusen, translated by Carol A. Flath. New Press, 1995, pp. 291–331.

Prentiss, Elizabeth. *Stepping Heavenward.* Collins' Clear-Type Press, 1869.

Qiu, Miaojin. *Notes of a Crocodile.* 1994. Translated by Bonnie Huie. NYRB, 2017.

Quintero, Isabel. *Gabi: A Girl in Pieces.* Cinqo Punto Press, 2014.

Ray, Annie. Diary, 1881–84 (excerpts). *The Extraordinary Work of Ordinary Writing: Annie Ray's Diary.* Edited by Jennifer Sinor. U Iowa P, 2002.

Richardson, Samuel. *Pamela; or Virtue Rewarded.* 1740. Edited by Peter Sabor. Penguin Classics, 1981.

Rosenberg, Alfred. Diary, 1936–44. U.S. Holocaust Memorial Museum. https://collections.ushmm.org/search/catalog/irn73077

Rowson, Susanna. *Sincerity.* 1803–04. Edited by Duncan Faherty and Ed White. *Just Teach One*, no. 7, Fall 2015. http://jto.common-place.org/just-teach-one-homepage/rowsons-sincerity-1803-04/

Russell, Rachel Renée. *Dork Diaries: Tales From a Not-So-Fabulous Life.* Aladdin, 2009.

Sansal, Boualem. *The German Mujahid.* Translated by Frank Wynne. Europa Editions, 2008.

Sarton, May. *As We Are Now.* W.W. Norton, 1973.

Sartre, John-Paul. *Nausea.* 1938. Introduced by Hayden Carruth, translated by Lloyd Alexander. New Directions, 1964.

Saunders, George. "The Semplica Girl Diaries." *Tenth of December.* Random House, 2013, pp. 109–67.

Singh, Amar. *Reversing the Gaze: Amar Singh's Diary, A Colonial Subject's Narrative of Imperial India.* Edited by Susanne Hoerber Rudolph, Lloyd I. Rudolph, and Mohan Singh Kanota. 2nd Edition. Oxford UP, 2000.

Smith, Dodie. *I Capture the Castle.* St. Martin's Griffin, 1948.

Smith, L.J. *The Vampire Diaries.* Vol. 1: *The Awakening.* Hodder Children's Division, 2010.

Smithsonian Digital Volunteers: Transcription Center, Smithsonian Institution. https://transcription.si.edu/

Smy, Pam. *Thornhill.* Roaring Brook Press, 2017.

Snyder, Susan. *Beyond Words: 200 Years of Illustrated Diaries.* Bancroft Library, U California Berkeley, 2011.

Sontag, Susan. *As Consciousness Is Harnessed to Flesh: Journals and Notebooks, 1964–1980.* Edited by David Rieff. Picador, 2012.

———. *Reborn: Journals and Notebooks, 1947–1963.* Edited by David Rieff. Farrar Strauss Giroux, 2008.

Stoker, Bram. *Dracula.* 1897. Penguin, 2003.

Sugawara no Takasue no Musume. *The Sarashina Diary: A Woman's Life in Eleventh-Century Japan.* Edited and translated by Sonja Arntzen and Moriyuki Itō. Columbia UP, 2018.

Tamaki, Mariko and Jillian Tamaki. *Skim.* Groundwood Books, 2010.

Tanizaki, Junichiro. *The Key and Diary of a Mad Old Man.* 1961, 1962. Translated by Howard Hibbert. Vintage, 2004.

Thistlewood, Thomas. *Diaries, 1750–1786.* Thomas Thistlewood Papers, Beinecke Library, Yale U. http://brbl-dl.library.yale.edu/vufind/Search/Results?lookfor=OSB_MSS_176&type=CallNumber&sort=title

Thoreau, Henry David. *The Journal of Henry D. Thoreau.* Edited by Bradford Torrey and Francis H. Allen. 14 vols. Houghton Mifflin, 1949.

Townsend, Sue. *The Secret Diary of Adrian Mole, Aged 13 ¾.* 1982. Harper Perennial, 2010.

Trondheim, Lewis. *Les petites riens.* www.lewistrondheim.com/blog/

———. *Little Nothings 1: The Curse of the Umbrella.* NBM Publishing, 2008.

Turgenev, Ivan. *Diary of a Superfluous Man.* 1850. Translated by David Patterson. W.W. Norton, 1999.

Twain, Mark. *Innocents Abroad and Roughing It.* Library of America, 1984.

Vandermeer, Jeff. *Annihilation.* Farrar, Straus and Giroux, 2014.

Van Dyke, Rachel. *To Read My Heart: The Journal of Rachel Van Dyke, 1810–1811.* Edited by Lucia McMahon and Deborah Schriver. U Pennsylvania Press, 2000.

Walker, Alice. *The Color Purple.* 1982. Mariner Books, 2003.

Warner-Vieyra, Myriam. *Juletane.* 1982. Translated by Betty Wilson. Waveland Press, 2014.

Woolf, Virginia. *The Diary of Virginia Woolf.* Edited by Anne Olivier Bell, assisted by Andrew McNeillie. 5 vols. Harcourt Brace Jovanovich, 1979–1985.

Wordsworth, Dorothy. *Home at Grasmere: Extracts from the Journal of Dorothy Wordsworth and from the Poems of William Wordsworth.* Edited by Colette Clark. Penguin, 1960.

Zhang, Jie. "Love Must Not Be Forgotten." 1979. *Love Must Not Be Forgotten.* Translated by Gladys Young. Panda Books, 1987, pp. 1–15.

Zhang, Xianliang. *Grass Soup.* Translated by Martha Avery and David R. Godine, 1995.

Secondary Works

Abbott, H. Porter. *Diary Fiction: Writing as Action.* Cornell UP, 1984.

———. "Letters to the Self: The Cloistered Writer in Nonretrospective Fiction." *PMLA* vol. 95, no. 1, 1980, pp. 23–41.

Achor, Shawn. *The Happiness Advantage: The Seven Principles of Positive Psychology that Fuel Success and Performance at Work*. Crown Business, 2010.

Adams, Timothy Dow. *Telling Lies in Modern American Autobiography*. U North Carolina P, 1990.

Altman, Janet Gurkin. *Epistolarity: Approaches to a Form*. Ohio State UP, 1982.

Ariès, Philippe. "Introduction." *The History of Private Life*. Edited by Philippe Ariès and Georges Duby. Vol. III: Passions of the Renaissance. Edited by Roger Chartier, translated by Arthur Goldhammer. Belknap Press of Harvard UP, 1989, pp. 1–11.

Askehave, Inger and Anne Ellerup Nielsen. "Digital Genres: A Challenge to Conventional Genre Theory." *Information Technology and People*, vol. 18, no. 2, 2005, pp. 120–41.

Babcock, Matthew J. "Learning Logs in Introductory Literature Courses." *Teaching in Higher Education*, vol. 12, no. 4, 2007, pp. 513–23.

Baker, Noelle A. "'Something more than material': Nonverbal Conversation in Mary Moody Emerson's Almanacks." *Resources for American Literary Study*, vol. 35, 2010, pp. 29–67.

Berger, Harry, Jr. "The Pepys Show: Ghost-Writing and Documentary Desire in 'The Diary.'" *ELH*, vol. 65, no. 3, 1998, pp. 557–91.

Bolter, Jay David and Richard Grusin. *Remediation: Understanding New Media*. MIT Press, 1999.

Bornstein, George. "Facsimiles and Their Limits: The New Edition of Yeats's *The Winding Stair and Other Poems*." *Textual Cultures: Texts, Contexts, Interpretation*, vol. 6, no. 2, 2011, pp. 92–102.

Brennan, Summer. "Notes from the Resistance: A Column on Language and Power." *Literary Hub*, 9 Dec. 2016. https://lithub.com/notes-from-the-resistance-a-column-on-language-and-power/

Bunkers, Suzanne L. "Diaries: Public and Private Records of Women's Lives." *Legacy*, vol. 7, no. 2, 1990, pp. 17–26.

Burnett, Bill and Dave Evans. *Designing Your Life: How to Build a Well-Lived, Joyful Life*. Knopf, 2016.

Buzzetti, Dino and Jerome McGann. "Critical Editing in a Digital Horizon." *Electronic Textual Editing*. Edited by John Unsworth, Katherine O'Brien O'Keeffe, and Lou Burnard. Text Encoding Initiative. www.tei-c.org/Vault/ETE/Preview/mcgann.html

Caplan, Nigel A. "Revisiting the Diary: Rereading Anne Frank's Rewriting." *Anne Frank's The Diary of Anne Frank*. Edited by Harold Bloom. Bloom's Literary Criticism, 2010, pp. 83–100.

Cardell, Kylie. *De@r World: Contemporary Uses of the Diary*. U Wisconsin P, 2014.

———. "The Future of Autobiography Studies: The Diary." *a/b: Auto/biography Studies*, vol. 32, no. 2, 2017, pp. 347–350.

———. "Modern Memory-Making: Marie Kondo, Online Journaling, and the Excavation, Curation, and Control of Personal Digital Data." *a/b: Auto/biography Studies*, vol. 32, no. 3, 2017, pp. 499–517.

Carter, Kathryn. "Accounting for Time in Nineteenth-Century Manuscript Diaries and Photographs." *Life Writing*, vol. 12, no. 4, 2015, pp. 417–30.

Carter, Paul J., et al. "Happy Thoughts: Enhancing Well-Being in the Classroom with a Positive Events Diary." *Journal of Positive Psychology*, vol. 13, no. 2, 2018, pp. 110–21.

Carvajal, Doreen. "Anne Frank's Diary Gains 'Co-Author' in Copyright Move." *New York Times*, 13 Nov. 2015. www.nytimes.com/2015/11/14/books/anne-frank-has-a-co-as-diary-gains-co-author-in-legal-move.html

Chambers, Ross. *Facing It: AIDS Diaries and the Death of the Author*. U Michigan P, 1998.

Cook, Matt. "Sex Lives and Diary Writing: The Journals of George Ives," *Life Writing and Victorian Culture*. Edited by David Amigoni. Ashgate, 2006, pp. 195–214.

Cottam, Rachel. "Diaries and Journals: General Survey." *Encyclopedia of Life Writing: Autobiographical and Biographical Forms*. Edited by Margaretta Jolly. 2 vols. Fitzroy Dearborn, 2001, pp. 267–69.

Couser, G. Thomas. "Genre Matters: Form, Force, and Filliation." *Life Writing*, vol. 2, no. 2, 2005, pp. 139–56.

Crangle, Sara. "Out of the Archive: Woolfian Domestic Economies." *Modernism/Modernity*, vol. 23, no. 1, 2016, pp. 141–76.

Cummings, H. R. "Barbellion's Diaries: A Reply." *History*, n.s., vol. 6, October 1921, pp. 183–94.

Day, Sara K. *Reading Like a Girl: Narrative Intimacy in Contemporary American Young Adult Literature*. UP Mississippi, 2013.

Delafield, Catherine. *Women's Diaries as Narrative in the Nineteenth-Century Novel*, Ashgate, 2009.

Derrida, Jacques. *Archive Fever: A Freudian Impression*. Translated by Eric Prenowitz. U Chicago P, 1995.

Didion, Joan. "On Keeping a Notebook." *Slouching Towards Bethlehem*. Dell, 1961, pp. 131–41.

Dijck, José van. *Mediated Memories in the Digital Age*. Stanford UP, 2007.

Doll, Dan. "'Like Trying to Fit a Sponge into a Matchbox': Twentieth-Century Editing of Eighteenth-Century Journals." *Recording and Reordering: Essays on the Seventeenth- and Eighteenth-Century Diary and Journal*. Edited by Doll and Jessica Munns. Bucknell UP, 2006, pp. 211–28.

Eakin, Paul John. *Fictions in Autobiography: Studies in the Art of Self-Invention*. Princeton UP, 1985.

———. *Living Autobiographically: How We Create Identity in Narrative*. Cornell UP, 2008.

Eggert, Paul. "Apparatus, Text, Interface: How to Read a Printed Critical Edition." *The Cambridge Companion to Textual Scholarship*. Edited by Neil Fraistat and Julia Flanders. Cambridge UP, 2013, pp. 97–118.

Felski, Rita. *The Limits of Critique*. U Chicago P, 2015.

Ferriter, Meghan. "Volunpeers: Hashtag, Identity, and Collaborative Engagement." *Meghan in Motion*. 5 April 2016. http://meghaninmotion.com/2016/04/05/volunpeers-hashtag-identity-engagement/

Filgate, Michele. "Will Social Media Kill Writers' Diaries?" *Salon*, 4 Aug. 2013. www.salon.com/2013/08/04/will_social_media_kill_the_writers_diary/

Fothergill, Robert A. *Private Chronicles: A Study of English Diaries*. Oxford UP, 1974.

Foucault, Michel. *The Archeology of Knowledge and the Discourse on Language*. Translated by A. M. Sheridan Smith. Pantheon, 1972.

———. *Discipline and Punish: The Birth of the Prison*. Translated by Alan Sheridan. Vintage, 1977.

———. *The History of Sexuality: Vol 1: An Introduction*. Translated by Robert Hurley. Vintage, 1990.

Frattaroli, Joanne. "Experimental Disclosure and Its Moderators: A Meta-Analysis." *Psychological Bulletin*, vol. 132, no. 6, 2006, pp. 823–65.

Fuchs, Miriam. "The Diaries of Queen Lili'uokalani." In *Significance of Primary Records*. Modern Language Association, 1995. www.mla.org/Resources/Research/Surveys-Reports-and-Other-Documents/Publishing-and-Scholarship/Significance-of-Primary-Records/Read-the-Report-Online/The-Diaries-of-Queen-Lili-uokalani-Miriam-Fuchs

Fuentes, Marisa J. *Dispossessed Lives: Enslaved Women, Violence, and the Archive*. U Pennsylvania P, 2016.

Gabler, Hans Walter. "Theorizing the Digital Scholarly Edition." *Literature Compass*, vol. 7, no. 2, 2010, pp. 43–56.

Garbarini, Alexandra. *Numbered Days: Diaries and the Holocaust*. Yale UP, 2006.

Garvey, Ellen Gruber. *Writing with Scissors: American Scrapbooks from the Civil War to the Harlem Renaissance*. Oxford UP, 2012.

Gasster, Susan. "Inside Looking Out: The Journal Novel in West African Francophone Literature." *Modern Language Studies*, vol. 23, no. 3, 1993, pp. 60–72.

Gay, Peter. *Education of the Senses*. Vol. 1 of *The Bourgeois Experience: Victoria to Freud*. Norton, 1984.

Genette, Gérard. *Paratexts: Thresholds of Interpretation*. Translated by Jane E. Lewin, foreword by Richard Macksey. Cambridge UP, 1997.

Gilman, William H. "Introduction." *The Journals and Miscellaneous Notebooks of Ralph Waldo Emerson*. Edited by Gilman, Alfred R. Ferguson, George P. Clark, and Merrill R. Davis. Vol. 1. Belknap Press of Harvard UP, 1960, pp. xiii–l.

Gordon, Bryony. "Dear Diary, I'm Glad to Find You're Still Alive." *The Telegraph*, 14 Jan. 2013. www.telegraph.co.uk/women/mother-tongue/familyadvice/9800532/Dear-Diary-Im-glad-to-find-youre-still-alive.html

Gunner, Liz. "Keeping a Diary of Visions: Lazarus Phelalasekhaya Maphumulo and the Edendale Congregation of AmaNazaretha." *Africa's Hidden Histories: Everyday Literacy and Making the Self*. Edited by Karin Barber. Indiana UP, 2006, pp.155–79.

Gusdorf, Georges. "Conditions and Limits of Autobiography." *Autobiography: Essays Theoretical and Critical*. Translated by James Olney. Edited by Olney. Princeton UP, 1980, pp. 28–48.

Hampsten, Elizabeth. *Read This Only to Yourself: The Private Writings of Midwestern Women, 1880–1910*. Indiana UP, 1982.

Hardwick, Elizabeth. "Memoirs, Conversations and Diaries." *View of My Own: Essays in Literature and Society*. Farrar, Straus and Cudahy, 1962, pp.49–65.

Harrison, Kimberly. *The Rhetoric of Rebel Women: Civil War Diaries and Confederate Persuasion*. Southern Illinois UP, 2013.

Hassam, Andrew. "Reading Other People's Diaries." *University of Toronto Quarterly*, vol. 56, no. 3, 1987, pp. 435–42.

———. *Writing and Reality: A Study of Modern British Diary Fiction*. Greenwood Press, 1993.

Hellbeck, Jochen. *Revolution on My Mind: Writing a Diary Under Stalin*. Harvard UP, 2006.

Herring, Susan C., Lois Ann Scheidt, Elijah Wright, and Sabrina Bonus. "Weblogs as a Bridging Genre." *Information Technology and People*, vol. 18, no. 2, 2005, pp. 142–71.

Hogan, Rebecca. "Endangered Autobiographies: The Diary as a Feminine Form." *Prose Studies*, vol. 14, no. 2, 1991, pp. 95–107.

Hoogenboom, Hilde. "The Famous White Box: The Creation of Mariia Bashkirtseva and Her Diary." *Gender and Sexuality in Russian Civilisation*. Edited by Peter I. Barta. Routledge, 2001, pp. 181–204.

hooks, bell. *remembered rapture: the writer at work*. Holt, 1999.

Huff, Cynthia A. "Reading as Re-Vision: Approaches to Reading Manuscript Diaries." *Biography,* vol. 23, no. 3, 2000, pp. 504–23.

Humphreys, Lee. *The Qualified Self: Social Media and the Accounting of Everyday Life*. MIT Press, 2018.

Hunter, J. Paul. *Before Novels: The Cultural Contexts of Eighteenth-Century English Fiction*. W.W. Norton, 1990.

Hunter, Jane H. "Inscribing the Self in the Heart of the Family: Diaries and Girlhood in Late-Victorian America." *American Quarterly*, vol. 44, no. 1, 1992, pp. 51–81.

Hutchinson, Conner. "The Lost Art of Keeping a Diary." *The Boar*, 15 Nov. 2017. https://theboar.org/2017/11/lost-art-keeping-diary/

Huxford, Grace. "'Write Your Life!': British Prisoners of War in the Korean War (1950–1953) and Enforced Life Narratives." *Life Writing*, vol. 12, no. 1, 2015, pp. 3–23.

Kagle, Steven E. and Lorenza Gramegna. "Rewriting Her Life: Fictionalization and the Use of Fictional Models in Early American Women's Diaries." *Inscribing the Daily: Critical Essays on Women's Diaries*. Edited by Suzanne L. Bunkers and Cynthia A. Huff. U Massachusetts P, 1996, pp. 38–55.

Karns, Christina M., William E. Moore III, and Ulrich Mayr. "The Cultivation of Pure Altruism via Gratitude: A Functional MRI Study of Change with Gratitude Practice." *Frontiers in Human Neuroscience*, vol. 11, 2017, pp. 1–14.

Kennedy, Helen. "Beyond Anonymity, or Future Directions for Internet Identity Research." Poletti and Rak, pp. 25–41.

Kitzmann, Andreas. *Saved From Oblivion: Documenting the Daily from Diaries to Web Cams*. Peter Lang, 2004.

———. "That Different Place: Documenting the Self Within Online Environments." *Biography*, vol. 26, no. 1, 2003, pp. 48–65.

Kropf, Evyn C. "Will that Surrogate Do?: Reflections on Material Manuscript Literacy in the Digital Environment from Islamic

Manuscripts at the University of Michigan Library." *Manuscript Studies*, vol. 1, no. 1, 2016, pp. 52–70.

Kuhn-Osius, K. Eckhard. "Making Loose Ends Meet: Private Journals in the Public Realm." *German Quarterly*, vol. 54, no. 2, 1981, pp. 166–76.

Kumbier, Alana. *Ephemeral Material: Queering the Archive*. Litwin Books, 2014.

Kunin, Aaron B. "Other Hands in Pepys's Diary." *MLQ*, vol. 65, no 2, 2004, pp. 195–219.

Lange, Patricia G. "Publicly Private and Privately Public: Social Networking on YouTube." *Journal of Computer-Mediated Communication*, vol. 13, 2008, pp. 361–80.

Lejeune, Philippe. "The Autobiographical Pact." *On Autobiography*. Edited by Paul John Eakin, translated by Katherine Leary. U Minnesota P, 1989, pp. 3–30.

———. *On Diary*. Edited by Jeremy D. Popkin and Julie Rak, translated by Katherine Durnin. U Hawaii P, 2009.

Lester, David. *The 'I' of the Storm: Understanding the Suicidal Mind*. De Gruyter, 2014.

Levine, Robert M. and José Carlos Sebe Bom Meihy. "Introduction." *The Unedited Diaries of Carolina Maria de Jesus*. Edited by Levine and Meihy, translated by Nancy P. S. Naro and Cristina Mehrtens. Rutgers UP, 1999, pp. 1–17.

Malhotra, Anshu and Siobhan Lambert-Hurley. "Introduction." *Speaking of the Self: Gender, Performance, and Autobiography in South Asia*. Edited by Anshu Malhotra and Siobhan Lambert-Hurley. Duke UP, 2015, pp. 1–30.

Manoff, Marlene. "Theories of the Archive from Across the Disciplines." *Portal: Libraries and the Academy*, vol. 4, no. 1, 2004, pp. 9–25.

Martens, Lorna. *The Diary Novel*. Cambridge UP, 1985.

Marwick, Alice E. and danah boyd. "Networked Privacy: How Teenagers Negotiate Context in Social Media." *New Media and Society*, vol. 16, no. 7, 2014, pp. 1051–67.

Matthews, William. "The Diary." *The Diary of Samuel Pepys, 1660–1669*. Edited by Robert Latham and William Matthews. Vol. I. U California P, 1970, pp. xli–lxvii.

———. "The Diary as History." *The Diary of Samuel Pepys, 1660–1669*. Edited by Robert Latham and William Matthews. Vol. I. U California P, 1970, pp. cxiv–cxxxvii.

———. "The Diary as Literature." *The Diary of Samuel Pepys, 1660–1669*. Edited by Robert Latham and William Matthews. Vol. I. U California P, 1970, pp. xcvii–cxiii.

Mbodj-Pouye, Aïssatou. "Writing the Self in Rural Mali: Domestic Archives and the Genres of Personal Writing." *Africa*, vol. 83, no. 2, 2013, pp. 205–26.

McCarthy, Molly. *The Accidental Diarist: A History of the Daily Planner in America*. Chicago UP, 2013.

McMahon, Lucia. "'We Would Share Equally': Gender, Education, and Romance in the Journal of Rachel Van Dyke." *To Read my Heart: The Journal of Rachel Van Dyke, 1810–1811*. Edited by Lucia McMahon and Deborah Schriver. U Pennsylvania Press, 2000, pp. 309–37.

McNeill, Laurie. "Brave New Genre, or Generic Colonialism? Debates over Ancestry in Internet Diaries." *Genres in the Internet: Issues in the Theory of Genre*. Edited by Janet Giltrow and Dieter Stein. John Benjamins, 2009, pp. 144–61.

———. "Labelling Our Selves: Genres and Life Writing." *Life Writing*, vol. 2, no. 2, 2005, pp. 7–18.

———. "Life Bytes: Six-Word Memoir and the Exigencies of Auto/tweetographies." Poletti and Rak, pp. 144–164.

———. "There is no 'I' in Network: Social Networking Sites and Posthuman Auto/Biography." *Biography*, vol. 35, no. 1, 2012, pp. 65–82.

McNeill, Laurie and John D. Zuern. "Online Lives 2.0." *Biography*, vol. 38, no. 2, 2015, pp. v–xlvi.

Medway, Peter. "Fuzzy Genres and Community Identities: The Case of Architecture Students' Sketchbooks." *The Rhetoric and Ideology of Genre: Strategies for Stability and Change*. Edited by Richard Coe, Lorelei Lingard, and Tatiana Teslenko. Hampton Press, 2002, pp. 123–53.

Miller, Carolyn R. "Genre as Social Action." *Quarterly Journal of Speech*, vol. 70, 1984, pp. 151–67.

Miller, Rachel Wilkerson. "Here's Why Teens Keep Diaries." *Buzzfeed*, 20 Aug. 2017. www.buzzfeed.com/rachelwmiller/teens-on-why-they-keep-a-diary

Moffat, Mary Jane and Charlotte Painter, eds. *Revelations: Diaries of Women*. Vintage, 1975.

Moody, Glyn. "Copyright Chaos: Why Isn't Anne Frank's Diary Free Now?" *Arstechnica.com*, 26 April 2016. https://arstechnica.com/tech-policy/2016/04/anne-frank-diary-copyright-public-domain/

Moon, Jennifer A. *Learning Journals: A Handbook for Reflective Practice and Professional Development*. 2nd edition. Routledge, 2006.

Moran, Joe. "Private Lives, Public Histories: The Diary in Twentieth-Century Britain." *Journal of British Studies*, vol. 54, 2015, pp. 138–62.

Morrison, Aimée. "Facebook and Coaxed Affordances." Poletti and Rak, pp.112–31.

Mumford, Louis. "Emerson Behind Barbed Wire." *New York Review of Books*, 18 January 1968, pp. 3–5.

Nardi, Bonnie A., Diane J. Schiano, and Michelle Gumbrecht. "Blogging as Social Activity, or Would You Let 900 Million People Read Your Diary?" *Proceedings of Computer-Supported Cooperative Work 2004*, vol 6, no. 3, 2004, pp. 222–31.

Neufeldt, Leonard N. "Thoreau in his Journal." *The Cambridge Companion to Henry David Thoreau*. Edited by Joel Myerson. Cambridge UP, 1995, pp. 107–23.

Nicholson, Bob. "The Digital Turn: Exploring the Methodological Possibilities of Digital Newspaper Archives." *Media History*, vol. 19, no.1, 2013, pp. 59–73.

Nolan, Maura. "Medieval Habit, Modern Sensation: Reading Manuscripts in the Digital Age." *Chaucer Review*, vol. 47, no. 4, 2013, pp. 465–76.

Nussbaum, Felicity. "Toward Conceptualizing Diary." *Studies in Autobiography*. Edited by James Olney. Oxford UP, 1988, pp. 128–40.

O'Connell, Timothy S. and Janet E. Dyment. "The Case of Reflective Journals: Is the Jury Still Out?" *Reflective Practice*, vol. 12, no. 1, 2011, pp. 47–59.

Page, Ruth E. *Stories and Social Media: Identities and Interaction*. Routledge, 2012.

Paperno, Irina. "What Can Be Done with Diaries?" *Russian Review*, vol. 63, no. 4, 2004, pp. 561–73.

Pascal, Roy. *Design and Truth in Autobiography*. Routledge, 1960.

Patterson, David. *Along the Edge of Annihilation: The Collapse and Recovery of Life in the Holocaust Diary*. U Washington P, 1999.

Pinsent, Pat. "Sacred Texts: The Role of Diary Passages in Recent Children's Fiction." *Journal of Children's Literature Studies*, vol. 3, no. 2, 2006, pp. 80–99.

Pitcan, Mikaela, Alice E. Marwick, and danah boyd. "Performing a Vanilla Self: Respectability Politics, Social Class, and the Digital World." *Journal of Computer-Mediated Communication*, vol. 23, 2018, pp. 163–79.

Podnieks, Elizabeth. *Daily Modernism: The Literary Diaries of Virginia Woolf, Antonia White, Elizabeth Smart, and Anaïs Nin.* McGill-Queen's UP, 2000.

Poletti, Anna and Julie Rak. *Identity Technologies: Constructing the Self Online.* U Wisconsin P, 2014.

Pollard, A. F. "An Essay in Historical Method: The Barbellion Diaries." *History*, n.s, vol. 6, April 1921, pp. 23–32.

Pollitt, Katha. "Review of Anaïs Nin's *Incest.*" *New York Times*, 22 Nov. 1992, pp. BR3. Proquest Historical Newspapers.

Porte, Joel. "Preface." *Emerson in His Journals.* Edited by Porte. Belknap Press of Harvard UP, 1982, pp. v–xi.

Pratt, Mary Louise. *Imperial Eyes: Travel Writing and Transculturation.* Routledge, 1992.

Prince, Gerald. "The Diary Novel: Notes for the Definition of a Sub-Genre." *Neophilologus*, vol. 59, 1975, pp. 477–81.

Prose, Francine. *Anne Frank: The Book, the Life, the Afterlife.* Harper Collins, 2009.

Punday, Daniel. "From Synesthesia to Multimedia: How to Talk about New Media Narrative." *New Narratives: Stories and Storytelling in the Digital Age.* Edited by Ruth Page and Bronwen Thomas. U Nebraska P, 2011, pp. 19–34.

Rak, Julie. "The Digital Queer: Weblogs and Internet Identity." *Biography*, vol. 28, no.1, 2005, pp. 166–82.

Raoul, Valerie. "Women's Diaries as Life-Savings: Who Decides Whose Life Is Saved? The Journals of Eugénie de Guérin and Elisabeth Leseur." *Biography*, vol. 24, no. 1, 2001, pp. 140–51.

Reynolds, Dwight F. "The Fallacy of Western Origins." *Interpreting the Self: Autobiography in the Arabic Literary Tradition.* Edited by Reynolds. U California P, 2001, pp. 17–35.

Rimmon-Kenan, Shlomith. *Narrative Fiction: Contemporary Poetics.* Methuen, 1983.

Rosenwald, Lawrence. *Emerson and the Art of the Diary.* Oxford UP, 1988.

Rudolph, Susanne Hoerber, Lloyd I. Rudolph, and Mohan Singh Kanota. "Introduction." *Reversing the Gaze: Amar Singh's Diary, A Colonial Subject's Narrative of Imperial India.* Edited by Rudolph, et al. 2nd Edition. Oxford UP, 2000, pp. 3–44.

Schwartz, Joan M. and Terry Cook. "Archives, Records, and Power: The Making of Modern Memory." *Archival Science*, vol. 2, 2002, pp. 1–19.

Serfaty, Viviane. *The Mirror and the Veil: An Overview of American Online Diaries and Blogs.* Rodopi, 2004.

Shandler, Jeffrey. "From Diary to Book: Text, Object, Structure." *Anne Frank Unbound: Media, Imagination, Memory*. Edited by Barbara Kirshenblatt-Gimblett and Jeffrey Shandler. Indiana UP, 2012, pp. 25–58.

Sherman, Stuart. *Telling Time: Clocks, Diaries, and English Diurnal Form, 1660–1785*. U Chicago P, 1996.

Shilling, Jane. "What Point the Secret Diary in the Instagram Age?" *The Telegraph*, 30 July 2017. www.telegraph.co.uk/news/2017/07/30/point-secret-diary-instagram-age/

Siemens, Ray, et al. "Towards Modeling the Social Edition: An Approach to Understanding the Electronic Scholarly Edition in the Context of New and Emerging Social Media," *Literary and Linguistic Computing*, vol. 27, no. 4, 2012, pp. 445–61.

Simons, Judy. *Diaries and Journals of Literary Women from Fanny Burney to Virginia Woolf*. U Iowa P, 1990.

Simsek, Omer Faruk. "Self-Absorption Paradox is Not a Paradox: Illuminating the Dark Side of Self-Reflection." *International Journal of Psychology*, vol. 48, no. 6, 2013, pp. 1109–21.

Sinor, Jennifer. *The Extraordinary Work of Ordinary Writing: Annie Ray's Diary*. U Iowa P, 2002.

Skeehan, Danielle C. "Caribbean Women, Creole Fashioning, and the Fabric of Black Atlantic Writing." *The Eighteenth Century*, vol. 56, no. 1, 2015, pp. 105–23.

Smith, Roger. "Self-Reflection and the Self." *Rewriting the Self: Histories from the Renaissance to the Present*. Edited by Roy Porter. Routledge, 1997, pp. 49–57.

Smith, Sidonie and Julia Watson. *Reading Autobiography: A Guide for Interpreting Life Narratives*. 2nd edition. U of Minnesota, 2001.

Sorapure, Madeleine. "Screening Moments, Scrolling Lives: Diary Writing on the Web." *Biography*, vol. 26, no. 1, 2003, pp. 1–23.

Spacks, Patricia Meyer. *Privacy: Concealing the Eighteenth-Century Self*. U Chicago P, 2003.

Steedman, Carolyn. "Enforced Narratives: Stories of Another Self." *Feminism and Autobiography: Texts, Theories, Methods*. Edited by Tess Cosslett, Celia Lury and Penny Summerfield. Routledge, 2000, pp. 25–39.

Stein, Daniel and Anthony M. Grant. "Disentangling the Relationships Among Self-Reflection, Insight, and Subjective Well-Being: The Role of Dysfunctional Attitudes and Core Self-Evaluation." *Journal of Psychology*, vol. 148, no. 5, 2014, pp. 505–22.

Steinitz, Rebecca. *Time, Space, and Gender in the Nineteenth-Century British Diary*. Palgrave MacMillian, 2011.

Stoler, Ann Laura. *Along the Archival Grain: Epistemic Anxieties and Colonial Common Sense*. Princeton UP, 2009.

———. "Colonial Archives and the Arts of Governance." *Archival Science*, vol. 2, 2002, pp. 87–109.

Tate, Claudia. Contribution to "The Inevitability of the Personal" Forum. *PMLA*, vol. 111, no. 5, 1996, pp. 1147–48.

Thain, Marion. "Digitizing the Diary: Experiments in Queer Encoding." *Journal of Victorian Culture*, vol. 21, no. 2, 2016, pp. 226–41.

Trubek, Anne. *The History and Uncertain Future of Handwriting*. Bloomsbury, 2016.

Vermeer, Leonieke. "Tiny Symbols Tell Big Stories: Naming and Concealing Masturbation in Diaries (1650–1940)." *European Journal of Life Writing*, vol. 6, 2017, n.p. https://doi.org/10.5463/ejlw.6.209

Walker, Janet A. "Reading Genres Across Cultures: The Example of Autobiography." *Reading World Literature: Theory, History, Practice*. Edited by Sarah Lawall. U Texas Press, 2010, pp. 203–34.

Warren, Michelle R. "The Politics of Textual Scholarship." *The Cambridge Companion to Textual Scholarship*. Edited by Neil Fraistat and Julia Flanders. Cambridge UP, 2013, pp. 119–33.

Watson, Julia. "Visual Diary as Prosthetic Practice in Bobby Baker's Diary Drawings." *Biography*, vol. 35, no. 1, 2012, pp. 21–44.

Webster, Tom. "Early Stuart Puritanism." *The Cambridge Companion to Puritanism*. Edited by John Coffey and Paul C. H. Lim, Cambridge UP, 2008, pp. 48–66.

Whitlock, Gillian and Anna Poletti. "Self-Regarding Art." *Biography*, vol. 31, no. 1 2008, pp. v–xxiii.

Wiener, Wendy J. and George C. Rosenwald. "A Moment's Monument: The Psychology of Keeping a Diary." *The Narrative Study of Lives*. Edited by Ruthellen Josselson and Amia Lieblich. Sage, 1993, pp. 30–58.

"Will Diaries be Published in 2050?" *The New York Times*. 25 Nov. 2012 www.nytimes.com/roomfordebate/2012/11/25/will-diaries-be-published-in-2050

Williams, Zoe. "Me! Me! Me! Are We Living through a Narcissism Epidemic?" *The Guardian*, 2 Mar. 2016. www.theguardian.com/lifeandstyle/2016/mar/02/narcissism-epidemic-self-obsession-attention-seeking-oversharing

Wolf, Hope. "'Paper Is Patient': Tweets from the '#AnneFrank of Palestine.'" *Textual Practice*, vol. 29, no. 7, 2015, pp. 1355–74.

Woolf, Virginia. "John Evelyn." *The Essays of Virginia Woolf*, Vol. III: 1919–1924. Edited by Andrew McNeillie. Hogarth Press, 1988, pp. 259–68.

Zamudio-Suaréz, Fernanda. "Why Historians Want You to Journal in the Age of Trump." *The Chronicle of Higher Education*, 31 May 2017. www.chronicle.com/article/Why-Historians-Want-You-to/240214

Zimmerman, Jess. "Social Media Is Our Modern Diary. Why Do Tech Companies Own All the Keys?" *The Guardian*, 21 Oct. 2014. www.theguardian.com/commentisfree/2014/oct/21/social-media-tech-companies-user-privacy

Zimroth, Evan. "The Sex Diaries of John Maynard Keynes." *The Gay and Lesbian Review*, vol 15, no. 4, 2008, pp. 19–20.

Zuern, John. "Online Lives." *Biography*, vol. 26, no. 1, 2003, pp. v–xxv.

Index

Note: The page numbers in *italics* refer to figures.

Affinity (Waters) 100
al-Radi, Nuha 76–7
Alexander, Jeb 39–40
Amiel, Henri-Frédéric 54, 165
analog diary *see* diary
Annihilation (Vandermeer) 102–3
anonymous diaries 136–7; and feeling anonymous online 140; *see also* digital diaries; truth
archive, the 26–30
As We Are Now (Sarton) 108
autobiographical fiction 96
"autobiographical I" 65; and collective representation 153
autobiographical pact 63; *see also* diary pact
autobiography: diary compared with 62–3, 68, 80
autobiography studies: and the diary 12–13, 62–3, 126, 160
autofiction *see* autobiographical fiction

Barbellion, W. N. P. 71, 78–9, 125, 165
Bashkirtseff, Marie 12, 73–4
beginnings: of diaries 77–8; and diary fiction 115
The Blazing World (Hustvedt) 111
blogs 8, 21, 127, 129–32, 134–7; *see also* digital diaries
Bobak, Molly Lamb 82, *83*
born digital diaries *see* digital diaries
Boswell, James 54, 77, 165
Browning, Elizabeth Barrett 71

chronology *see* diary time
codes *see* diary codes
codes of concealment 92; *see also* diary codes
codes of convenience 91; *see also* diary codes
collaborative diaries 72; *see also* diary readers
The Collector (Fowles) 108
colonialism: and the diary 27–9; and diary fiction 118–19
comics *see* diary comics
concealments: in diaries 84–8; *see also* diary codes
The Counterfeiters (Gide) 106
critical editions 43–7

Dang, Thuy Tram 4–5
Davis, Emilie 50–1
de Guérin, Eugénie 72
de Jesus, Carolina Maria 42

"dear diary" 69–70
diaries addressed to limited readers 70–1; *see also* diary readers
diaries addressed to the public 73–4; *see also* diary readers; published diaries
diarist-narrator: in diary fiction 106–9
diarists: reasons for writing 150–1; reasons for writing in diary fiction 115
diary: categories of 7–9; defining 4–7; future of 146–9; history of 9–15; myths about 1–2, 20, 73, 145, 147–8; versus journal 2–3
Diary (Palahniuk) 110
diary apps 8, 129, *130*, 134, 139, 146; *see also* digital diaries
diary as literature 60–3; *see also* genre paradox
diary codes 56, 72, 87–8, 91–4
diary comics 122; *see also* graphic narrative
diary conventions *see* beginnings, concealments, diary readers, diary subject, diary time, endings, image, middleness, silences
diary fiction: colonialism and postcolonialism in 118–19; definitions of 95–6; and graphic narrative 121–4; history of 97–101; and nonfiction diaries 95, 124–5; sex, gender, and sexuality in 117–18; and young adult fiction 119–21
diary hoaxes 127, 137
diary manuscripts: in diary fiction 101–6; and digital diaries 133–5; reading 30–5
diary narrators *see* diarist-narrator
diary novel *see* diary fiction
The Diary of a Good Neighbor (Lessing) 106
"Diary of a Madman" (Gogol) 99
"Diary of a Madman" (Lu) 99
Diary of a Mad Old Man (Tanizaki) 99
"Diary of a Superfluous Man" (Turgenev) 99
Diary of a Wimpy Kid (Kinney) 3, *3*
Diary of the Fall (Laub) 116
diary pact 63; *see also* autobiographical pact
diary readers 68–74; and digital diaries 141–2, 143–4; emotional responses of 15–17; ethical obligations of 15, 154, 156
diary subject 64–8; and digital diaries 135–8; and self-construction 160–1
diary time 10, 75–7; and diary fiction 113–6; and digital diaries 142–4
The (Diblos) Notebook (Merrill) 103
Didion, Joan 127
digital diaries: affordances of 131; commercialization of 142; compared to analog diaries 129–32, 145–6; and the diary subject 135–8; different forms of 128–9; versus digitized diaries 48, 129, 134
digital materiality 133; *see also* digital diaries
digitized diaries *see* digitized editions
digitized editions 48–52
"The Distances" (Cortázar) 99–100
Dracula (Stoker) 98, 114
Drinker, Elizabeth 79–80, 91
Duncan-Wallace, A. M. 86

Edith's Diary (Highsmith) 109
editor-reader: in diary fiction 109–13
education: and diary writing 162–5; sample assignment *163*
educational diary *see* education

Either/Or (Kierkegaard) 110–11
Emerson, Mary Moody 32–3, *33*
Emerson, Ralph Waldo 45–6
empowerment: and diary writing 156–7
endings: of diaries 78–9; and diary fiction 115–16
enforced narrative 157–8
enslaved people: and the diary 27–8
epistolary fiction 97
Erasure (Everett) 100
Everyone Leaves (Guerra) 108

Facebook 128, 138, 146, 147
facsimile editions 35–6
family-edited editions 39–41
feminist approaches to the diary 12, 17, 29, 54–8
femininity *see* feminization of the diary
feminization of the diary 54–8, 156–7; in diary fiction 117–18; and educational diaries 165; *see also* gender paradox; women writers
Field, Michael 66
Filipović, Zlata 20, 70
foreign language in diaries *see* diary codes
framing narratives: in diary fiction 109–11
Frank, Anne 12, 40–1, 69–70, 120, 127
Frank, Otto 40–1
Fujii, Takuichi 82–4, *85*; *see also* Japanese American diaries
Fun Home (Bechdel) *123*
future, of the diary 146–9

gay writers *see* LGBTQ writers
gender *see* diary fiction; feminization of the diary; gender paradox; women writers
gender paradox 12–13, 55–8
genre paradox 60–3; and gender paradox 62
The German Mujahid (Sansal) 115
Gide, André 54, 98, 106
Gillespie, Emily Hawley 56
Gobetti, Ada 92
Gombrowicz, Witold 64, 67
Gone Girl (Flynn) 104–5
graphic memoir *see* graphic narrative
graphic narrative: and diary fiction 121–4
graphic novel *see* graphic narrative
graphomania 165; *see also* psychology
gratitude journal 8, 162, 169
Grimké, Charlotte Forten 77
Guevara, Ernesto "Che" 76

handwritten manuscripts 23, 30–2, *33*, 147; and digital diaries 133–5; decline of 147; *see also* diary manuscripts
A Hero of Our Time (Lermontov) 99, 108–9
Hillesum, Etty 68–9
historical documentation: and diary writing 151–4
HIV/AIDS: and the diary 155–6
Hoby, Lady Margaret 12
Holocaust diaries 15, 153–4, 159; and diary fiction 116; and diary hoaxes 127
Hooke, Robert 91, 135
hooks, bell 156–7
Houseboy (Oyono) 110

"if a book is locked there's probably a good reason for that don't you think?" (Oyeyemi) 100
illustrated diaries 82–4, *83*, *85*
image: in the diary 82–4; *see also* illustrated diaries

impermanence: of digital diaries 134
indoctrination: and diary writing 158
Inman, Arthur 75, 165
The Innocents Abroad (Twain) 114
involuntary diaries 138; in education 165
Iphigenia (de la Parra) 108
The Izumi Shikibu Diary 100; *see also* Japanese diaries

Japanese American diaries 50, 82–4, *85*
Japanese diaries: history of 14; and diary fiction 100
journal letters *see* letter diaries
The Journal of Albion Moonlight (Patchen) 103
Journal of The Counterfeiters (Gide) 106
journal versus diary 2–3
Julavits, Heidi 77, 169

Kaplan, Chaim A. 153–4
Keynes, John Maynard 93

Lejeune, Philippe *see* autobiographical pact
lesbian writers *see* LGBTQ writers
letter diaries 71–2, 97
LGBTQ writers 12, 39, 57, 66, 93–4, 155–6
limited-address diaries *see* diaries addressed to limited readers
Lister, Anne 93
literariness of the diary *see* diary as literature
Livingstone, David 50–1
Lolita (Nabokov) 99
Lu, Xun 99

"mad diarist" motif 99
Manguso, Sarah 76, 165
manuscripts *see* diary manuscripts
marked silences *see* silences
"material manuscript literacy" 34; and digitized diaries 49
mediated editions 41–3
mediated self 136; *see also* digital diaries
menstruation: in diaries 55–6, 91
mental health: and diary writing 160–2, 164–6
Michaels, Eric 155
Michitsuna no Haha 14; *see also* Japanese diaries
middleness: in diaries 79–80; in diary fiction 113; and digital diaries 143; *see also* diary time
middles of diaries, *see* middleness
misreading diaries 88–90
The Moonstone (Collins) 98
motive *see* diarists

narcissism: and diary writing 67, 69, 148, 150; and digital diaries 140
Nausea (Sartre) 99, 102
networked readers 141–2; *see also* diary readers
Ngubane, Thembi 156
Nin, Anaïs 37–8, 66, 127
Nini, Rachid 5
Nineteen Eighty-Four (Orwell) 102
nonfiction diary *see* diary
nonretrospective diary 62, 76; in diary fiction 114
non-Western diaries 13–15; and diary fiction 118–19
The Notebooks of André Walter (Gide) 98–9
Notes from the Underground (Dostoevsky) 99

obsolete *see* future
ordinary diaries 61–2
oversharing: and digital diaries 140, 148

Pamela (Richardson) 98
panopticon 158
parataxis 79
paratexts 81
paths to readers 24, *25*
Pavese, Cesare 127, 165
Pepys, Elisabeth 12
Pepys, Samuel 10–11, 12, 54, 90, 92–3
permanence: of digital diaries 134
personal criticism 17
Plath, Sylvia 165
Podlubny, Stepan Filippovich 86
politics: diary writing as 151–9; limits of 158–9
A Portrait of the Artist as a Young Man (Joyce) 99
Possession (Byatt) 100
postcolonialism *see* colonialism
privacy: alternate terms for 21; and the diary 19–22; and digital diaries 139–42; and published diaries 19; and risk 141–2
psychologizing *see* misreading diaries
psychology: and diary writing 160–2, 164
public privacy *see* privacy
published diaries 19, 37–8, 73–4, 109; analog versus digital 143; influence on diarists 11, 124; *see also* privacy

Queen Lili'uokalani 32

Ray, Annie 56, 91
readers *see* diary readers
rematerialization: of digital diaries 134
remediation: and digital diaries 131
Renzi, Emilio 66
revision: of digital diaries 137; *see also* truth
risk: of digital diaries 141–2
Robinson Crusoe (Defoe) 97, 108
rumination: and diary writing 164, 166

The Sea, The Sea (Murdoch) 114
scenes of composition: in diary fiction 102
scenes of discovery: in diary fiction 102
self-addressed diaries 68–9; *see also* diary readers
self-edited editions 36–9
self-help: and diary writing 160, 162
self-rhetoric: in the diary 67
"The Semplica Girl Diaries" (Saunders) 100
sex: in the diary 39, 55–6, 57, 92–4; in diary fiction 117–18; *see also* diary codes
sexuality *see* sex
silences: in diary 84–8
Sincerity (Rowson) 98
Singh, Amar 29
single-author epistolary novels 97; *see also* diary fiction
snippetotomy *see* misreading diaries
social editions 50
social media: and the diary 128–30, 134, 137–42, 146–9
Sontag, Susan 161
The Sorrows of Young Werther (Goethe) 98
space: in the diary 80–1; *see also* illustrated diaries
Stepping Heavenward (Prentiss) 107
story of the found document 110–11; *see also* scenes of discovery
storying *see* misreading diaries
Sugawara no Takasue no Musume 14; *see also* Japanese diaries

suicide: and diary writing 165–6
"Susy L—'s Diary" (Cate) 112

A Tale for the Time Being (Ozeki) 104
The Tenant of Wildfell Hall (Brontë) 98
text-addressed diaries 69–70; *see also* diary readers
Thistlewood, Thomas 27–8
Thoreau, Henry David 4, 54, 65
time *see* diary time
The Tosa Diary 100; *see also* Japanese diaries
truth: and the diary 125–7; and digital diaries 136–7, 143; and revision of digital diaries 137
truthfulness *see* truth
Twitter 128, 135, 143

unliterary, diary defined as *see* diary and literature
unmarked silences *see* silences

Van Dyke, Rachel 72
vlogs 8, 129; *see also* digital diaries

Western bias: and diary history 13–15, 28–9; and diary fiction 118–19
writers of color: and the diary 28–9, 41–2, 62, 156–7
women writers: and the diary 12–13, 54–8, 62, 156–7; *see also* feminization of the diary; gender paradox
Woolf, Leonard 56, 79
Woolf, Virginia 4, 37, 56, 79, 165
Wordsworth, Dorothy 87–8
working class writers: and the diary 12, 41–2, 50, 62

Young adult fiction: and diary fiction 119–21

Zhang, Xianliang 92

For Product Safety Concerns and Information please contact our EU representative GPSR@taylorandfrancis.com
Taylor & Francis Verlag GmbH, Kaufingerstraße 24, 80331 München, Germany

www.ingramcontent.com/pod-product-compliance
Lightning Source LLC
Chambersburg PA
CBHW070536100726
47907CB00004B/1141

* 9 7 8 0 4 1 5 7 8 9 2 0 2 *